THE
CHICANO
HERITAGE

HISPANOS
AND
AMERICAN POLITICS

Daniel Valdes y Tapia

ARNO PRESS

A New York Times Company

New York — 1976

Editorial Supervision: LESLIE PARR

———◆———

First publication in book form, 1976
  by Arno Press Inc.

Copyright © 1964 by Daniel Valdes y Tapia

THE CHICANO HERITAGE
ISBN for complete set: 0-405-09480-9
See last pages of this volume for titles.

Manufactured in the United States of America

———◆———

Library of Congress Cataloging in Publication Data

Valdes y Tapia, Daniel, 1916-
   Hispanos and American politics.

   (The Chicano heritage)
   Reprint of the author's thesis, University of
Colorado, 1964.
   Bibliography: p.
   1. Mexican Americans--Politics and suffrage.
I. Title. II. Series.
E184.M5V26 1976   324'.2   76-1613
ISBN 0-405-09531-7

HISPANOS AND AMERICAN POLITICS

A SOCIOLOGICAL ANALYSIS AND DESCRIPTION
OF THE POLITICAL ROLE, STATUS, AND VOTING BEHAVIOR
OF AMERICANS WITH SPANISH NAMES

By

DANIEL VALDES Y TAPIA, PH.D.

PREFACE

Hundreds of books, monographs, and articles dealing with the role and relationship of racial and cultural minorities to the total social structure have been published in the United States in the last two decades. Most of the studies have been of a particularistic nature, each minority group has been studied by itself, or they have been highly specialized with reference to the concepts and explanatory principles which they employ. This has often led to oversimplified, one-factor views of dominant-minority relations. Greater attention should be paid in the study of dominant-minority relations to the connection between studies in this field and the findings, concepts, and theories of the behavioral sciences. Dominant-minority relations cannot be properly understood as an isolated or unique phenomenon. Every concept and theory concerning dominant-minority relations should be a part of general concepts and principles on intergroup relations. It is not enough to understand prejudice or the place of minorities in the social structure. It is also necessary to understand the types of social interaction, the functions of institutions, and the meaning of culture in dominant-minority relations.

Some of the writings in the field have been uncritical of the sources of their material, have too easily assumed the usefulness of the concepts employed, and have engaged in causal inferences that have not been fully justified. There exists a need for more carefully controlled studies in dominant-minority relations, more tentative statements, and a greater use of qualifying statements if we are to take account of the methodological and logical problems involved. Previous studies of minority groups and their relation to the larger society have already served to show that the position which each of these groups holds in the total social structure could be put in conceptual terms similar enough to warrant designating and describing their positions in terms of a dominant-minority relationship. The social sciences have started to make generalizations about the characteristics of a minority and to describe typical processes involved in the relation of the minority to the dominant group. In the last twenty years, these aspects of intergroup relations has become a recognized special field of sociology. Sociological studies have discarded or challenged older concepts and theories as an ever-increasing body of research findings has thrown new light on the subject. For example, one of the most pervasive of the older theories, that assimilation is the inevitable goal of the dominant-minority process, is now being re-examined in the light of the new concept of cultural pluralism in private aspects of life and pluralistic economy and democracy in public life.

The central unit of investigation of this thesis is not minorities or even a minority as such but the relation of one minority, the Hispanos, to the dominant group in selected areas of the United States in certain political situations. The hypothesis-testing portion of the report involves the major problem to which this study is directed, which is the direct assessment of the basic concept of ethnic consciousness and how it is related to voting behavior in specific dominant-minority situations.

This dissertation represents an attempt to provide, through a carefully controlled study, empirical data on dominant-minority relations in specified situations and to interpret these data in terms of concepts and theories on intergroup relations, as developed by the behavioral sciences. It goes further than this, however, for an attempt is made to formulate general principles that might apply to any dominant-minority relations under a given set of circumstances. In this way we hope to have added to the research findings in the field and also to have made a contribution toward the development of more valid theories of dominant-minority relations. There is no finality to our findings or conclusions, but no science can or should give the impression of finality.

The writer acknowledges with gratitude, the advice, direction, and encouragement of Professors Robert Hansen, Judson Pearson, Blaine Mercer, Merle Adams, and especially, Professor Alex Garber. The writer also wishes to acknowledge the assistance and encouragement of Dolores Valdes, who did a masterly job of typing this manuscript. Finally, he wants to thank the following interviewers for interest and effort "beyond the call of duty": Gerald Fine, John Dikeou, Larry De Credico, Priscilla Pino, Dolores Valdes, LeRoy Hagen, and Anthony Zamora.

NOTE ON TERMINOLOGY:

The term "Hispano" is a cultural term used in the U.S. Southwest to designate persons with Hispanic backgrounds. As such, it embraces descendents of the old Spanish colonists, whether of pure Spanish or of mixed

Spanish and Indian ancestry, as well as persons of Spanish or Spanish-Indian ancestry who more recently have immigrated to the United States from the Republic of Mexico. The term, "Anglo" is used to designate all persons other than Hispanos, Indians, Negroes, or Orientals.

The term "dominant" is the reciprocal of the term "minority" and is used instead of "majority" because it carries with it the connotation of superordination and superior power which "majority" does not convey.

TABLE OF CONTENTS

073115

LIST OF TABLES

LIST OF FIGURES

CHAPTER I

INTRODUCTION

There is a rather widely held assumption that the Hispano in the United States is becoming increasingly interested and active as an Hispano in the political life of many American communities and on the state-wide level, at least, in the states of New Mexico, California, Texas, and Colorado.

In the present study, this assumption is quite well established as correct by an analysis of voting statistics in two important recent elections, one in Colorado and the other in Texas. Whether the Hispano's growing political importance and his tendency to vote as an Hispano (rather than as a Democrat or Republican, as a Catholic or Protestant or as a poor man or rich man) is due to an awakening ethnic consciousness or to political "manipulation" by special interest groups (such as the Teamster's Union in Crystal City, Texas or by political parties such as in the Kennedy presidential campaign of 1960) has not been studied or established.

The study and analysis of this idea of ethnicity and its relation to voting behavior, the degree of exposure to selected mass media communication and social-economic factors is the central theme of this dissertation. It belongs both in the category of sociological historical investigation and analysis and to the category of hypothesis testing. The historical treatment and voting analysis based on election statistics involve several of those southwestern states in which the Hispano constitutes a substantial proportion of the total population.[1] Also, since voting behavior cannot be divorced from the community and culture that produces it, part of the study is a descriptive analysis of the historical and present-day social and economic status of the Hispanic people of the Southwest and the role they have played and are now playing in the politics of these states. See Table I for the number of persons with Spanish surnames in various states in the United States Southwest.

The panel research survey, which is an important part of this dissertation, constitutes an attempt to measure ethnic consciousness in the Hispanos in the City and County of Denver, to relate this "consciousness" to the dependent variable, voting behavior, and to see if and how, in a particular localized election, this "consciousness," or to use a more acceptable sociological concept, in-group identification, translates itself into effective political action.

In addition, the panel survey method is used to analyze the predispositions and stimuli to which this population was subjected during the Denver mayoralty election of 1963. By repeated interviewing of the same respondents selected from a representative sampling of Americans with Spanish surnames over a period of time, it was possible to overcome the limitations and obstacles posed by purely ecological studies and those presented by studies based solely upon precinct election results.

---

[1]Colorado, 13%; New Mexico, 38%; Texas, 23%; California, 15%.

3

TABLE I

NUMBER OF WHITE PERSONS WITH SPANISH SURNAMES
IN THE UNITED STATES SOUTHWEST*

State	1960	1950
Arizona	194,356	128,318
California	1.426,538	760,453
Colorado	157,173	118,131
New Mexico	269,122	248,880
Texas	1.417,811	1,033,768

*White persons of Spanish surname in the United States Southwest, where the Hispano-American population is concentrated, numbered 3,465,000, according to the 1960 Census of Population figures. This an increase of 1,175,450, or 51.3 per cent, over the figure of 2,289,550 reported in the 1950 Census of Population.

The major problem to which this study is directed, is the direct
assessment of the basic concept of ethnic consciousness, and how it is
related to voting behavior. Sociologists have, for some time, stressed
that an individual's conduct is affected by his "assessment of the situation," the "social frame of reference." Why not investigate what Hispanos think and feel about "being Spanish" and how these feelings influence them when it comes to voting? A person's ethnicity can be measured
by what he thinks and feels as well as by his associations and behavior.
The basic concept of ethnic consciousness or ethnicity has been used before as an interpretative device, but as far as this writer has been able
to discover, no effort has ever been made to measure it directly among
American Hispanos. Certainly, no panel survey has ever been conducted
for the purpose of measuring this concept directly or for discovering if
there is any significant correlation between ethnicity and voting behavior
in a specific situation, in which the degree of exposure to selected mass
media communication (designed to arouse ethnicity) can also be directly
measured and correlated with the other factors.

To translate the concept of "ethnic consciousness" into empirical
research procedures, it was necessary to make three specifications:

1. A concrete sphere of action was selected, in this case
   voting behavior in the 1963 mayoralty contest, to which
   the concept could be related.
2. The idea of "ethnic consciousness" is too vague: a specific ethnic group had to be selected, in this case, Americans with Spanish surnames in the City and County of Denver.
3. A technique for measuring degrees of ethnicity had to be
   used. The same had to be done for the other major concept,
   the degrees of exposure to selected mass media communication.

The hypotheses to be tested may be summarized as follows:

1. Hispano oriented Americans with Spanish surnames will support ethnically acceptable candidates to a greater degree than Anglo oriented Americans with Spanish surnames.
2. Hispano oriented Americans with Spanish surnames with high exposure to ethnic propaganda will support ethnically acceptable candidates to a greater extent than Anglo oriented Americans with Spanish surnames also with high exposure to ethnic propaganda.
3. These Americans who are Hispano oriented will show a greater interest and intention to vote in an election charged with ethnic overtones to an extent greater than these Americans who are Anglo oriented.
4. The Hispano oriented among these Americans who have had high exposure to ethnic propaganda will show a greater interest and intention to vote than Anglo oriented Americans with Spanish surnames who also have had high exposure to ethnic propaganda.

To secure data to test these hypotheses, a sample of registered voters with Spanish surnames in the City and County of Denver was interviewed twice during the election for mayor in 1963 and once immediately after the election. On the basis of pertinent parts of these data, Guttman-type scales were constructed in order to determine whether the questions relative to ethnicity and exposure to ethnic propaganda were, in fact, related to these two variables and secondly, to rank the respondents along these two variables. Then, on the basis of this ranking, the respondents were divided into four groups: respondents with low ethnicity, respondents with high ethnicity, respondents with high exposure to ethnic propaganda, and respondents with low exposure to ethnic propaganda. After these four categories of the population were established, tests were administered to analyze the relationship between each of these groups and the groups in combination (high ethnicity, high exposure to ethnic propaganda, etc.), interest and intention to vote in the mayoralty election, and the manner in which each of the groups changed in their choice of mayoralty candidates.

This dissertation consists of six major divisions: (1) a general introduction, (2) a theoretical orientation, (3) the historical and contemporary setting of the problem and the population, (4) an analysis of the voting statistics in recent elections in two states with important Hispano populations, (5) a panel research survey which involves a sample of Hispanos in the City and County of Denver who were registered to vote in the Denver mayoralty election of May, 1963, and (6) an interpretation of the findings, and a summary followed by conclusions. The first chapter contains the general introduction, the next two chapters comprise a theoretical orientation, a critical review of the literature, and the background to the study of political phenomena. The fourth chapter contains a brief historical background which is necessary for the adequate understanding of the phenomena under study and is mainly an historical review of the status and role of the Hispanos in politics and government in those states originally settled by them and where they still constitute an important segment of the population. The fifth chapter brings us up to date on the political role and status of this ethnic group in the geographical areas covered. The next three chapters are devoted to the presentation of the specific research project undertaken and carried out for this study. It consists of the research design and the various phases of the research project; the findings, conclusions,

and interpretation of the findings are reviewed at the macroscopic **level**
and related to present—day political **roles** and **statuses of the Hispanos**
in Southwestern United States.

CHAPTER II

THEORETICAL ORIENTATION

The Concept of Race or Ethnic Consciousness and the Doctrine of Race
Determinism.

The dominance of some groups of human beings over other groups
goes back to antiquity, but the distinctive form of dominant-minority
relations characterized by "race or ethnic consciousness" is a modern
phenomenon. New patterns of dominant-minority relations have emerged
in modern history, all partially shaped by the penetration of other continents by white explorers, conquerors, and colonizers, who, in various
ways and in differing degrees, established hegemony over many of the
peoples who lived on these continents. The very word "race" came into
use in the 17th and 18th centuries when the struggle for markets and
colonies began on a vast scale. The exploitation of the natives, which
accompanied the acquisition of empires, was justified by the argument
that the white race was superior to the colored races and that its
mission was to civilize them.

Toward the middle of the 19th century, some sociologists and
other social scientists began to use biological concepts, such as "natural selection" and "survival of the fittest," as illustrations and ration-
alizations of the competitive processes underlying early capitalist economy. They started to interpret social phenomena in terms of these concepts and to bring them forward to prove that certain races were superior
to others and that class distinctions were inevitable. The organismic

conception of a social organism led to the glorification of race and the view that it is the main determinant in human progress.

But at the time that Charles Darwin was still hesitantly outlining his theories in The Origin of Species, which had referred to "The Preservation of Favored Races in the Struggle for Life,"[1] the idea of racial destiny had already been used by American expansionists to support the conquest of Mexico.[2] The dogma of the superiority of the "Anglo-Saxon race" became the chief element in American racism during its imperialistic era. Like other varieties of racism, Anglo-Saxonism was a product of modern nationalism and the romantic movement, rather than the outgrowth of biological science. The idea of "manifest destiny" had been invoked before 1859, when Darwin's work was first published. However, Darwinism was later used to bolster racist theories and as a new instrument in the hands of theorists of race struggles, although there was never anything in Darwinism that inevitably made it an apology for racist theories.

The early sociological foundation of racist theories and doctrines rests upon Gobineau's Essai sur l'Inegalite' des Races Humaines.[3] This

---

[1]Charles Darwin, The Origin of Species (New York: D. Appleton and Company, 1897), subtitle.

[2]Julius W. Pratt, "The Idealogy of American Expansion," Essays in Honor of William E. Dodd (Chicago: University of Chicago Press, 1935), p. 344, cited by Richard Hofstadter, Social Darwinism in American Thought (Revised Edition, Boston: The Beacon Press, 1955), pp. 171-172.

[3]Adrian Collins (trans.) Arthur de Gobineau: The Inequality of Human Races (New York: G. P. Putnam's Sons, 1915)

landmark in the history of Aryanism, which was published in 1853, was
not based on the idea of natural selection, but rather on cultural evolution, and, as such, was considered to be the mainspring of racial
theory in sociology. Gobineau believed that racial circumstances domin-
ated all major problems of history. He probably did not realize it,
but he inadvertantly introduced less restrictive connotations to the
term race, since he never explicitly stated what constituted a race and
confused race with ethnic groups. Sociology now has facts that show that
racial (or ethnic mixtures) sometimes result in the blossoming of cultures
and not in retrogression, as Gobineau contended, but Gobineau's racial
theories, although wrong and not widely circulated, served as a basis for
the work of Houston Stuart Chamberlain in Germany at the end of the 19th
century. Chamberlain's racial doctrines and theories were subsequently
adopted by Nazism and also helped the development of Anglo-Saxonism so
prevalent in the United States in the late 19th and early 20th-century
period.[4]

Six years before the publication of Darwin's theories, Herbert
Spencer had advanced the view that the pressure of subsistence upon population has a beneficial effect upon the human race and that this pressure
had stimulated human advancement and selected the best of each generation
for survival.[5] Indeed, it was Spencer who coined the phrase "survival

---

[4]Houston Stuart Chamberlain, Foundations of the Nineteenth
Century, cited by Nicolas S. Timasheff, Sociological Theory (Revised
Edition, New York: Random House, 1957), p. 51.

[5]Herbert Spencer, The Principles of Sociology (New York:
D. Appleton, 1897), p. 51.

of the fittest." But it remained for Ludwig Gumplowicz's books,
especially his Outlines of Sociology, to give the greatest impetus to
the racist basis to the sociology of races.[6] He believed that social
and cultural evolution is entirely a product of the struggle between
social groups and that groups fought because insurmountable hatred and
no communality of inheritance exists between groups and races.

Franklin H. Giddings contributed to theories in the sociology
of minorities by emphasizing the principle of "consciousness of kind,"
a phrase which he coined but which was based on the idea put forward by
Adam Smith, who, in his Theory of Moral Sentiments,[7] had noted the
importance of reflective sympathy in social life. According to Giddings,
consciousness of kind is a state of consciousness in which any being
recognizes another conscious being as of like kind.[8] He maintained that
social composition is the natural product of the physiological and psychological activities of individuals, supplemented by natural selection.
Groupings arise unconsciously. The simplest grouping included in the
concept of social composition is the family. Through the combination

---

[6]F. W. Moore (trans.), Ludwig Gumplowicz, Outlines of Sociology
(Philadelphia: American Academy of Political and Social Sciences, 1899),
pp. 76-82, p. 134 ff.

[7]Adam Smith, The Theory of Moral Sentiments (New York: G. P.
Putman's Sons, 1904), p. 168.

[8]F. W. Giddings, Principles of Sociology (New York: The Macmillan
Company, 1896), p. 17, p. 71.

of families, two broader types of groupings arise, one ethnic, the other
demotic (held together by habitual intercourse, mutual interests, and
cooperation, rather than kinship). In Giddings' sociology, the unit of
investigation is the socio or man related to other men through consciousness of kind.[9]

The Sociological Significance of Race and Ethnicity

Biologically, the conception of race is that of a permanent variety
of mankind composed of individuals descended from a common ancestor, who
diverged, by mutation, from the previously existing racial type. A race
is a division inferior to a species, yet possessed by constant trans-
missible traits sufficiently pronounced to characterize it as a distinct
type. The distinguishing marks are of less constant character and of
less biological significance than the traits which divide animals into
species.

Briefly, the physical differences among racial groups (and even
more so among ethnic groups) are slight and biologically unimportant.
It has not been shown that the traits used by anthropologists in their
classifications bear any constant relation to cultural capacity; mental
differences among the racial groups have not been demonstrated. But the
physical and visible marks of race are of great social and cultural
significance. They differentiate between groups of people, and they
condition contact and interaction. Social attitudes may arise toward

---

[9]Ibid., p. 126 ff.

physical and biological, as well as cultural, traits. Each isolated racial group, and men of all racial and ethnic groups, look upon their own type as the only fully human form and tend to fear or despise men of other races and ethnic groups. In practically all places in the modern world the conspicuous marks of race, particularly skin color, are made the object of favorable or unfavorable estimation. They are the basis for differential treatment and for social and cultural exclusion.

Scientifically, racism is demonstrably false. But it is one of the obvious experiences of social living that false ideas can be as effective in shaping human behavior as accurate ones. Racism and ethnicity are only two of many reasons for group prejudice but they are, perhaps, the most important ones. It should be noted that group prejudice may have nothing to do with race, as such. It may be exhibited by members of the same race toward others in the race. The Italian-Americans sometimes exhibit prejudice against Irish-Americans, members of the same race but of different ethnic origin. Variations in "racial" attitudes such as variations on the "color question" and language differences indicate that political, economic, and cultural factors are involved similar to those found in the manifestations of the in-group against the out-group. However, ethnocentrism seizes upon distinguishable physical and cultural characteristics because of their high visibility and segregating value when antagonism and conflict characterize the relations between groups.

Ethnocentrism, according to Sumner, "...leads a people to exaggerate and intensify everything in their own folkways which is peculiar and which differentiates them from others."[10] In other words, Sumner believed that ethnocentrism is functional. If ethnocentrism is functional in promoting social control within a group, it can also be dysfunctional in relations between groups, according to Lundberg.[11] High ethnicity on the part of any group is likely to incur a certain hostility on the part of other groups. Sorokin says the same thing in these terms: "When and where each group in a multigroup society has its values different from those of the other minority groups and from those of the majority, when there is no common fund of values, ...there will be an abundance of antagonism between the different minority groups and between these and the majority group."[12]

William R. Catten, Jr. and Sung Chick Hong report data that sustains the hypothesis that majority hostility is associated with the appearance of ethnocentrism in minorities.[13] They maintain that one of the reasons that such a hypothesis does not often appear in sociological literature is due to difficulties in defining and measuring the relevant variables that indicate degrees of ethnicity. They ask, "How can we measure the ex-

---

[10]William Graham Sumner, Folkways (Boston: Ginn & Co., 1906), p. 13.

[11]George A. Lundberg, "Some Neglected Aspects of the Minorities' Problem," Modern Age, 2 (Summer, 1958) pp. 290-291.

[12]Pitirim A. Sorokin, "Comments on William F. Albright's 'Some Functions of Organized Minorities'", in Tyman Bryson, et al., editors, Approaches to National Unity (New York: Harper & Bros. 1945), p. 274.

[13]William R. Catten, Jr. and Sung Chick Hong, "The Relation of Apparent Minority Ethnocentrism to Majority Antipathy", in Raymond W. Mack, Race, Class, and Power (New York: American Book Company), 1964, p. 342.

tent to which the behavior of a given minority is ethnocentric? Such data
are not readily available either in census volumes, rating records, or the
usual public opinion survey reports."[14]

The Sociology of Minorities

A general science of "race relations" or dominant—minority relations is, perhaps, not possible since these constitute only a part of the
"science of intergroup relations." Therefore, dominant—minority relations
are but a specialized approach to basic patterns of social interaction,
social structuring and social processes. There has been no established
cohesive body of theory on dominant—minority relations, since sociological
studies with respect to these relations have been part of a search for
an adequate theoretical approach to the totality of intergroup relations.
This does not mean that we should not attempt to discover interrelated
propositions on several levels of generality that could more adequately
describe and explain dominant—minority relations, or that this specific
type of relations does not require separate analysis. It does mean that
any theory of minorities must develop within the context of the general
development of social theory. Behavior in any form of intergroup relations
must be explained in terms of group obligations, group—defined interests
and goals, role categories, and structural-functional concepts. Consequently, the major concepts which sociology has used to define, analyze, and
explain dominant—minority relations include such concepts as "values,"
which are the beliefs governing approved actions in a society, "norms" or

---

[14]Ibid., p. 343.

"expected behavior," "roles," which implicitly or explicitly define ways of carrying out functions in the society in accordance with the norms, and "status," which defines the relative position of a person or a group with regard to another person or group in the hierarchy of prestige. In other words, the aspects of the social structure in which dominant-minority relations come into focus are the value system, the institutional role behavior, and the status hierarchies.

The interaction between different groups is not only initiated and maintained within the structure, but this interaction is part of a continuous process of change. Three aspects of this process have been identified by sociologists: the historical process of changing mutual relations; the contemporary processes of stable interaction; and the characteristic processes of interaction in time of stress. Historically, the nature of the initial contact between groups is of great importance. This contact may be on the basis of having no preconceived image of each other, on the basis of trade or barter, or on the basis of conflict or conquest. Four major patterns of dominant-minority relations have arisen in modern times, each due to the special historical configuration of the time: the political annexation pattern, the colonial pattern, the slave pattern, and the immigration pattern.[15] The relationships based on these patterns then pass through stages of ecological, economic, religious, and political organization, in which new modes of dominance take the place of the old.

---

[15]For a detailed discussion of these patterns, see Charles F. Marden and Gladys Meyer, Minorities in American Society (Second Edition; New York: American Book Company, 1962), pp. 6-10.

The stable interrelations established between dominant groups and minority groups are usually defined within the traditional categories of cooperation, competition, and conflict. Cooperation usually follows a pattern in which each group plays clearly defined superordinate and sub-ordinate roles within a relatively stable and well defined social structure. Competition occurs usually in the economic and political spheres. There is always potential conflict in dominant-minority relations, and in times of stress brought about by economic upheavals or depressions, war or rapid political or social changes, the lines of conflict between dominant and minority groups are sharpened and processes of re-adjustment come to the fore. This conflict may be in the form of greater insubordination of the minority group, conflict between different minority groups, a rise in ethnicity, and the solidarity and cohesiveness of both the dominant and minority groups, thus accentuating the historical and contemporary differ-ences and conflicts between them.

Newer theories and assumptions in American sociology regarding dominant-minority relations have raised questions about older assumptions. Anthropology, psychology, and psychiatry also have developed theories of human behavior that are relevant to dominant-minority situations and have provided some insights which older theories did not provide. But since in this study we are not concerned with attitudes except as these attitudes affect the social system, we here discuss only the development of theories and insights developed by sociologists.

Robert E. Park up to fifteen years ago, was the most important contributor to sociological theory as it relates and applies to race and culture.[16] He tried to formulate generalizations within the context of general theories of society. Louis Wirth was Park's colleague in this attempt, and their joint contributions in this field came to be known as Park-Wirth school of thought on "race relations." Park's major contribution lies in his recognition and definition of the differences between prejudice and discrimination, his concept of the marginal man, and his belief that prejudice and discrimination rise in periods of social change. One major theory proposed by Park has been successfully challenged by more recent research. Contemporary writing challenges Park's contention that relations between dominant and minority groups move through a definite cycle, ending in inevitable assimilation of the minority into the dominant society. Park also felt that urbanization increased tension between groups, but more recent research indicates that this is not always true. Perhaps Park's and Wirth's greatest contribution lies in the fact that they provided concepts and insights upon which others could base their research and from which they could develop more valid sociological theories in the field of ethnic and race relations. Kimball Young and Raymond W. Mack redefined Park's concept of accommodation as a state of equilibrium between groups in which certain working arrangements have been agreed upon or accepted.[17] Subsequently, Charles F. Marden and Gladys Meyer stressed the fact that

---

[16]Robert E. Park, Race and Culture (Glencoe, Ill.: The Free Press, 1950).

[17]Kimball Young and Raymond W. Mack, Sociology and Social Life (2nd ed., New York: American Book Co., 1962), p. 489.

working arrangements must sometimes be accepted by the minority group.
They maintain that it is a mode of adaption about which the minority has
no choice and that it constitutes an adjustment by the minority to conditions over which it has no control.[18] Gunnar Myrdal adds to the development of the concept of accomodation by pointing out that accommodation
has both its external or behavioral element and the internal or attitudinal element.[19] This insight is founded on ample historical evidence that
much accommodation is external only.

The concept of acculturation, similar to Park's concept of assimilation, has been further developed in such contemporary writing as that
of Herskovits and Broom and Kitsuse, who have emphasized the situational
factor in acculturation.[20] In addition, Broom and Kitsuse pointed out
that a minority person's acceptance into the dominant groups must "vali-
date" his acculturation by the person being accepted in the major institutional patterns of the dominant group.[21] Another question which concerns

---

[18]Charles F. Marden and Gladys Meyer, Minorities in American
Society (Second Edition; New York: American Book Co., 1962), p. 424.

[19]Gunnar Myrdal, An American Dilemna (New York: Harper & Bros.
1944), p. 768.

[20]Melville J. Herskovits, Acculturation: The Study of Culture
Contact (Glouchester, Mass.: Peter Smith, 1958), p. 133; Leonard Broom
and John Kitsuse, "The Validation of Acculturation," American Anthro-
pologist, LVII (February, 1955), p. 44.

[21]Ibid, p. 44.

contemporary sociologists is the related problem of whether assimilation is the only goal of minority groups. Both Park and Wirth saw assimilation as the inevitable outcome, but Etzioni has challenged this view. He believes that in a pluralistic society, it is illogical not to include cultural pluralism.[22]

Sociological theory on minorities is increasingly making use of the concepts of status and role. It is a common assumption that ethnic identification is one of the factors affecting a position in the over-all status structure of a society, and both Broom and Kitsuse maintain that status competition is the crucial point of dominant-minority tension.[23] Role and role-behavior in older sociological theory on minorities was perceived as part of the problem of culture conflict.[24] This perception has been retained, developed, and refined by several writers on dominant-minority relations, including Lipset, who analyzed roles characteristic of situations found recurrently in comparable situations. Thus, Yankee traders in the South during reconstruction played marginal business roles which stereotyped them with traits associated with the Jewish stereotype.[25]

[22]Amitai Etzioni, "The Ghetto - A Re-evaluation," Social Forces, XXXVII (March, 1959), p. 255 ff.

[23]Broom and Kitsuse, op. cit., page 46.

[24]Oscar Handlin, The Uprooted (Boston: Little, Brown & Co., 1951).

[25] Seymour Martin Lipset, "Changing Social Status and Prejudice," p. 477, Social Problems, VI (Winter, 1958-1959), p. 253 ff.

Robert K. Merton has made significant contributions to the sociology of minorities within his now-famous "middle-range theory" category. By using W. I. Thomas' theorem that if men define situations as real, they are real in their results, Merton has pointed out that if this false definition is acted upon, it brings about a situation which fits the definition. He gave as an example the case of unions excluding Negroes because they have been strike breakers; then since they cannot join unions, they in fact become strike breakers.[26] When Park developed his concept of "marginality," his emphasis was on the conflict engendered in the personality by the attempt to internalize different sets of values inherent in the dominant and in the minority culture. For Merton the concept of marginality is a special instance of reference group theory. He sees it as behavior "in which the individual seeks to abandon one membership group for another to which he is socially forbidden access."[27]

Parson's further refinement and development of the concepts of status and role have given new and valuable insights into the problems of acculturation. One of his most valuable insights is his distinguishing between "universalistic" and "particularistic" values. He maintains that large-scale, complex technological societies have a much stronger value orientation toward universalistic norms (norms which apply equally to persons regardless of position) than a traditional folk society, and that

---

[26] Robert K. Merton, Social Theory and Social Structure (Revised edition; Glencoe, Ill.: The Free Press, 1957), p. 426.

[27] Robert K. Merton and Alice Rossi, "Contributions to the Theory of Reference Group Behavior" in Robert K. Merton's, Social Theory and Social Structure, op. cit., p. 266.

a person moving from one social system to another had to internalize not only the content of new values, but a new way of thinking, as between particularistic and universalistic values.[28]

Any analysis and interpretation of dominant—minority relations, it would appear, must take into account the combined interaction of many factors and social forces, including the principle of ethnicity or ethnocentrism and the principle of in-group—out-group interaction, historical circumstances, tradition, and the social forces inherent in the dynamics of industrial and political democracy.

Milton M. Gordon has recently written the first full-scale sociological survey of the assimilation of minority groups in America. In studying the racial, religious, and nationality or ethnic groups in the United States, he found a social organization more complex than can be described in terms of "cultural pluralism" or the "melting pot" concepts. He defines this organization as "structural pluralism." Social classes intersect with ethnic groups to form the decisive social units. According to Gordon, the American assimilation pattern has been one of massive acculturation or behavioral assimilation, as well as the maintenance of considerable structural separation. Gordon found evidence for these hypotheses in various empirical studies of racial, religious, and ethnic groups in the United States.[29]

---

[28]Talcott Parsons, Essays in Sociological Theory (Revised edition; Glencoe, Ill.: The Free Press, 1954), p. 395.

[29]Milton M. Gordon, Assimilation in American Life (New York: Oxford University Press, 1964) pp. 164-178.

Relevant Political Theories

The analysis of political processes and institutions has long
been a major concern of sociology, but sociologists recognize the fact
that it is impossible to study these phenomena except within an overall
sociological framework and more general sociological relationships.

The principal orientation of this thesis proceeds from a postu-
late of the political system as a social system or organization, rather
than as a mechanism or organism. As a social organization, it is the
way citizens in a society act. Organization, as a matter of fact, is
achieved through the stabilization and regularization of activity.
Activity is regularized or controlled in society by the working rules
(norms, laws, etc.) which define the limits within which individuals
may exercise their own wills. It should also be kept in mind that "own
wills" are really socially and culturally conditioned wills. Values are
conceived of as fundamentally institutional and relative to social organization. Freedom, for example, is not conceived of as a natural right;
rather, it is a social achievement.

The methodological approach suggested by this thesis permits the
researcher to analyze the constituent members of society which are the
subjects of all political action in any society. Insofar as man is a
social animal and, as such, is group-identified and expresses his social
needs through group action, the only valid basis upon which to analyze
political phenomena must be such groups.

Comparative studies of institutions and procedural arrangements are of value, but the limitation of their utility must be noted. Otherwise, one falls into the error of the political scientist of the past, who described the political world as if man were not a part of it. Man acts politically as a member of a group.

Although cultural norms do not fully account for regularities of behavior within groups and between groups, it is true that much of patterned human behavior is culturally prescribed. This is what we mean by institutionalized behavior. This also accounts for the emergence of subcultures. Norms develop peculiar to groups similarly situated in the social structure as in the professions and in unions among workers differently located in society and in ethnic contra-cultures that develop norms determining certain patterns of behavior. The impact of the contra-cultural group (characterized by a distinctive set of norms and values) is an important determinant of behavior.

A contra-cultural group is characterized by a large and complex combination of sets of norms, some of which are general cultural and some of which are distinctive to the contra-cultural group. These sets of normative patterns are always in conflict and/or in a state of accommodation. The degree of adherence to the distinctive norms of the contra-cultural group is measured by a person's awareness of being a part of an externally classified category of persons; his identification with the contra-cultural group; and, principally, by greater association with elements of the cultural group and adherence to ethnic attributes (attitudes, beliefs, and patterns of behavior) of his group.

Evaluating patterns of behavior, group structure and variation in values among contra-cultures must be taken into account. Behavior in intergroup or any group relations cannot be explained by what is "_in_" individuals, except as this might be taken to mean the _internalization_ of group norms, values, and beliefs. Men act in structured situations and behave in terms of their obligations and group-defined interests and goals.

Political institutions have evolved in response to a long development in political thought; but such political thought was, itself, primarily a response to historical, political, economic, and social developments--the very totality arising from the culture out of which such institutions evolved. In the political area, patterns of recruitment, decision-making, and administration reflect the comprehensive and dominant beliefs and interests of groups making up the culture or some compromise between conflicting beliefs and interests. Political institutions, in theory, at least, are attempts to regularize and legitimitize "rules" of political life and establish political institutions that will make such "rules" operative in culture. Parliamentarism, separation of powers, and civil rights, for example, find manifestation in specific political institutions designed to maximize their expression in political reality.

The whole system of political theories as developed in the 19th

and 20th centuries has been built upon the ideal of a perfect society of
liberty, equality, and fraternity among individuals, under the ideal name
of democracy, and not upon the more realistic and actual collective democracy of economic organizations and other special interest groups, such
as ethnic, racial, or religious categories.

Mountains of books have been written about political power and
political activity. Some writers have defied political power or torn it
from life itself. Some have expounded the logic and moral basis of the
state and glorified power. Others have maintained that it is essentially
immoral. Few have studied or been concerned with the role political power
plays in the process of social control and how, in turn, political power
is but one system within a larger system; consequently, few have applied
systems analysis to the phenomenon of political power. But new doctrines
of social environment, of social heritage (and even of personality), and
empirical research in such fields as economics, sociology, psychology, and
anthropology have appeared to upset older conceptions and conclusions.
Observations of social processes are yielding facts and interpretations
of great value in the understanding of current forms of political life.
Many of the secrets of political power are also found in the probe of
human personality, which, in turn, is a product of socialization.

A great error has been made in the past and continues to be made
by many political scientists in trying to distinguish political power
from other forms of power in social situations, such as power exercised
by the church, the private or economic association, or the labor union.
The attempt to draw such a sharp and exclusive line between political and

all other forms of organization has been fruitless and often confusing.
"What is the difference between economic power and political power,
between ecclesiastical power and political power, between group authority
in many forms and the more strictly political?" asks Charles Edward
Merriam, "the governmental, the political, all have their analogies in
other organizations, where similar phenomena of sub-, super-, and co-
ordination may be discovered—a clearer view is gained by frankly recog-
nizing the fundamental similarity between them, and the parallelism and
even frequent interchangeability of functions."[30]

In the 18th century, nationalism and capitalism challenged the
traditional systems of force, and once nationalism and capitalism acquired
stature and some measure of stability, political theories began to explain
the new phenomena on a rationalistic and naturalistic basis. This resulted
in efforts to explain the "state" on the basis of contractual agreements—
produced by conscious and rational decisions. Martindale states that it
was made "to rest upon 'human nature' and the powers of the individual in
yielding 'rational consent.' All political rights and duties were to be
derived from this source. Any variance from this principle in the actual
observed course of political conduct could only be due to factors prevent-
ing the full manifestation of human nature and reason."[31]

[30]Charles Edward Merriam, Political Power (New York: Whittlessey
House, McGraw-Hill Book Company, 1934), p. 8.

[31]Don Martindale, The Nature and Types of Sociological Theory
(Boston: Houghton Mifflin Company, 1960), p. 33.

Political theory based on the ideal state is still quite prevalent in political science, but as early as 1835, Alexis de Tocqueville pioneered a new kind of analysis based on the empirical examination of political phenomena within the context of social factors.[32] Others have visualized political theory as the theory of the causes, formations, and transformations of power.

Political Sociology

Political scientists did not even investigate individual action, much less the social or cultural roots of individual action, nor the variety of organized collective action controlling individual action. These in recent years have become the foundation of twentieth century political sociology. This new specialism in sociology recognizes that collective action proceeds, indeed, not from the intellectual logic of philosophers or political scientists, but rather from what has been called "community context," "structural contexts," and "structural effects."[33] These all designate all of the social influences upon individual political behavior, as well as collective political behavior--a person's social class position, his religious affiliation, national origin, sex, and age.

Political sociology was born in an atmosphere of argument as to what was more important, the state or society, and which preceded which.

---

[32] Alexis de Tocqueville, Democracy in America, Vol. 1 (New York: Vintage Books, 1954), pp. 9-11.

[33] William N. McPhee and William A. Glaser (eds.), Public Opinion and Congressional Elections (New York: The Free Press of Glencoe, The Macmillan Company, 1962), p. 181.

Saint Simon and Karl Marx believed that society was primary and the state must be controlled by society, whereas Hegel and Lorez von Stein believed in the supremacy of the state, subordinating social elements to the state. Although the debate of society versus the state is, for all practical purposes, a moot question, two important elements of the controversy still present important challenges to modern day political sociology. Lipset (in Merton's Sociology Today) says, "...The subjects of the controversy are no longer referred to as 'state' and 'society,' the underlying dilemma--that of the proper balance between conflict and consensus--continues."[34]

The problems of consensus and cleavage have been the focus of the study of politics, but sociologists have been much more concerned with social and cultural conditions making for conflict, rather than with conditions of political consensus. The writings of Marx, Tocqueville, Max Weber, and Michels attest to this fact. These were the men who founded and were the early great developers of political sociology. For Marx, conflict was primary in the study of politics. Although de Tocqueville proposed the conception of social systems involving a balance between the forces of conflict and consensus, he also emphasized the necessity of conflict among units of society. For Weber and Michels the central problem of modern politics is the relationship between bureaucracy and democracy.

---

[34]Lipset states that political science has matured as the "state" discipline and political sociology as the "radical" discipline, stressing social conflict and social change. See Merton, et al. (eds.), Sociology Today (New York: Basic Books, Inc., 1959), p. 83.

Lipset states that conflict, consensus, and bureaucracy are closely related,
since bureaucracy is one of the chief means of creating and maintaining
consensus.[35]

Major Theoretical Concepts

The major overall or general concepts (not necessarily operationally defined nor even explicitly dealt with in the thesis, but necessary
to a fuller understanding of the findings and interpretations contained
later in this thesis) are concepts which are implicit in any study of a
socio-political nature:

Social conflict. Two interrelated features of political action
appear in all political systems: the political units overtly or covertly
contending for political power; and the alleged purpose to which such
units wish to subordinate such political power. Several characteristics
of the political system, including structural or procedural characteristics, are significant with reference to those two features to the extent
that they operate to lend legitimacy of operation to a particular unit
or facilitate or impede participation of the unit in political life. It
is, of course, admitted that certain aspects of empirical reality will
operate to establish the capacity of any political unit to be effective
within any political system. At least seven aspects of that empirical
reality operate (usually in combination) to determine the conditions of

---

[35]Robert K. Merton, Leonard Broom, Leonard S. Cottrell, Jr.,
(eds.), Sociology Today (New York: Basic Books, Inc., 1959), p. 277.

effectiveness for political units or associations as well as interest groups:[36]

1. The numerical size of the unit in relation to the numerical size of all other political units in the system. This aspect may or may not be reflected organizationally, (e.g., Hispanos represent only 13 per cent of the population in Denver, but 65 per cent of the population in Santa Fe, New Mexico).

2. The capacity of such a unit to either neutralize or enlist the support of other units (e.g., in some areas, especially in Eastern cities, Jews, Negroes, and other minority groups work effectively together in politics).

3. The legitimacy to participate in political life accorded the unit (e.g., for nearly three quarters of a century, Hispanos in New Mexico were denied the right to vote for state officials). Also, the outlawing of Los Hermanos Penitentes several decades ago was more politically than religiously inspired.[37] This organization had been a potent force in local Colorado and New Mexico politics.

4. The prevailing institutional and procedural arrangements through which political demands are normally expressed (e.g., the poll tax in Texas until recently was an effective barrier against fuller political participation by Mexican-Americans in Texas politics).

5. The access of the political unit to instruments of persuasion or force such as the press, the educational system, radio, police, etc. (e.g., in nearly every area under study the Hispano lacks access to these instruments).

6. The quality of the leaders of the particular unit. This refers not only to the qualities of leaders, but also the status accorded such leaders in society (e.g., a new and more widely respected type of leader is emerging among the Hispanos).

7. The relationship of a political unit to forces exogamous to the society within which it operates (e.g., the cold war and more specifically our relations with Latin America are beginning to have an effect on Hispano-Anglo relations in the United States.

---

[36]Richard H. Pfaff, "The Effective Political Units in a Transitional Society" (University of Colorado, mimeographed).

[37]Condemned by Archbishop John B. Lamy in 1899.

Consensus. Tocqueville, unlike Marx, deliberately chose to emphasize the positive political aspects of social units which could maintain political cleavage and political consensus at the same time. He believed that private associations which are sources of restrictions on the
government also serve as major channels for involving people in politics,
and are mechanisms for creating and maintaining the consensus necessary
for a democratic society. Park and Burgess in Introduction to the Science
of Sociology[38] are most explicitly concerned with consensus. Louis Wirth
regards the study of consensus as the central task of sociology.[39] One
of the great proponents of the concept of consensus and its processes was
John R. Commons, whose views on social control in the introduction to his
great book, The Economics of Collective Action,[40] are reported in these
terms: "The common ground of all democratic (i.e., nonauthoritarian) control is...the procedures by which the wills of participants, including
those with conflicting interests, are brought together into a created
collective will." Commons' "collective will" is similar to Durkheim's
"collective consciousness." Lipset believes that viewing power as a facility or resource of the social system implies a concern with consensus as

[38]R. E. Park and E. W. Burgess, Introduction to the Science of
Sociology (second edition; Chicago: University of Chicago Press, 1924),
p. 163.

[39]Louis Wirth, "Consensus and Mass Communication," American
Sociological Review, XIII (February, 1948), 1-15.

[40]John R. Commons, The Economics of Collective Action (New York:
The Macmillan Company, 1950), p. 14 of the introduction by Kenneth H.
Parsons.

well as with struggle.[41]

The manner in which consensus is achieved, modified, or maintained in varying degrees differs widely depending on the political system, the circumstances, and the times. There are no elections in Cuba, yet few can deny that there have been degrees of consensus achieved (in earlier days of the Castro regime, consensus of the highest order), not at the ballot box in free elections but in massive public demonstrations of consensus. This was also true to a greater or lesser degree in Fascist Italy or Nazi Germany. But even in the most democratic (in the Western sense) nations, consensus is frequently achieved through numerous agencies of conciliation and arbitration. However, in this study, voting is the principal means of achieving and maintaining consensus and the concept of consensus is introduced only to highlight the fact that some degree of consensus is a necessary condition for social organization.

Voting is a key mechanism of consensus in democratic societies. For a number of decades, sociologists have been studying elections to discover and analyze the relationship between cleavage, political parties, and other sources of cleavage and conflict, such as class, occupation, religion, and ethnicity. A full discussion of this subject is found in Chapter III.

---

[41] Seymour Martin Lipset, "Political Sociology" in Robert K. Merton, Leonard Broom, and Leonard S. Cottrell, Jr. (eds.), Sociology Today (New York: Basic Books, Inc., 1959), pp. 81-114.

Social order. The basic issue of much of contemporary sociological analysis is the problem of order. Since this is the case, the stability or "orderliness" of political institutions appears to be the major concern of political sociology. In this connection, the topics of political sociology have been: electoral behavior, extremist political movements, bureaucracy, the internal government of voluntary associations, and power.

Power. The study of political power also highlights the difference between those who emphasize conflict or consensus. Parsons and Lynd[42] have pointed out that there are two basically different ways of looking at power, one of which is expressed by Parsons' "zero-sum" concept and Lynd's "scarcity theory." Both of these concepts assume that there is a limited or total sum of power. These theories, naturally, also assume that an increase in power for one group must occur at the expense of another. The other way of looking at power is to reject these concepts of power and look upon power as these writers do as "a facility for the performance of function in and on the behalf of the society as a system--(as) the capacity to mobilize the resources of the society for the attainment of goals for which a general 'public' commitment has been made or may be made."[43] This Parsonian and Lyndian concept of power is, in many respects, similar to Commons' "collective will" discussed above. Viewing power as a facility or resource of the social

---

[42]Robert S. Lynd, "Power in American Society as Resource and Problem," in Arthur Kornhauser (ed.), Problems of Power in American Society (Wayne University Press, 1957), p. 157.

[43]Ibid., p. 158.

system implies a concern with consensus as well as with struggle. Therefore, both Parsons and Lynd have done much to free power analysis from
identification with theories of conflict of interests.

Power is broadly considered to refer to the ability to determine
the behavior of others in accord with one's own wishes. Georg Simmel is
one among sociologists who have pointed out that the exercise of power involves an element of obedience, that it is more than the unilateral impo-
sition of will; it also involves acceptance.[44]

In a structural sense, the family of power is made up of not only
the state, the family, the church, business, and labor, but also of associations of all kinds. Among the most persistent of the associations which
demand representation are those based upon a pattern called "race," a vague
and relatively useless term, partly ethnic in nature and partly a cultural
pattern. It is used here to refer to a way of life transmitted to a group
as a social heritage. Important groupings of mankind cluster around group
patterns of behavior, group memories and hopes, language, values, and beliefs.

One of the primary purposes of this dissertation centers around an
analysis of the demands of racial and ethnic groups for political recognition or participation, ascertaining under what pressures these demands rise
and fall. Under what conditions does political recognition become an in-
dispensable part of the "race" urge, and on the other hand, what are the

---

[44]Georg Simmel, "Superiority and Subordination," American Journal
of Sociology; II (September, 1896), 394-415.

conditions under which this fades away, merged in another unity of emotional or interest appeal? The history and tactics of racial and cultural minorities are close to the problem of power, and the racial and cultural composition of the political community is of vital importance. Since these groups are also culture bearers, economic claims, religious interests, and other social demands are involved, all testing the elasticity of the political community and the toughness of the "racial" group.[45]

Racial and cultural groups do not uniformly develop political or other organizations of their own. Sometimes they hope for a flag of their own, as many Hispanos in the United States Southwest hoped during World Wars I and II. In the first World War, some hoped that Mexico would join Germany and launch an attack on the United States. In the second World War, some hoped that the Falange Movement would unite the whole of Hispanic America.[46] When that fails, racial or cultural groups may prefer their ghettos or their own courts. But usually, cultural and racial association are not highly organized, such as those found in the church or in industry or labor. Behind the singing society or the cultural center, there is some form of organization or government, but more loosely developed than the other types of the family of power. Under

[45]For studies of problems of multi-racial governments and political units, see Oscar Jaszi, The Dissolution of the Hapsburg Monarchy, Phoenix Paper Back 70, University of Chicago, 1957.

[46]The now almost defunct political arm of the world-wide Hispanic movement, sometimes known as Hispanidad.

certain circumstances a cultural group develops a highly organized, autono-
mous organization such as the "Fraternity of Our Father Jesus of Nazareth,"
most popularly known as <u>Los Penitentes</u>. For centuries it has been one of
the most important organizations of Hispanos in the American Southwest.[47]

The penalties of racial or cultural insubordination are no less
fearful and its rewards no less alluring than those of the other groups
that make up the family of power. The "race" may confer immortality and
fame on those it favors and enshrine them in poetry and song. No special
mechanism need exist for this purpose. Many of the Hispanos' most popular
<u>corridos</u>, folk songs that tell the story of a personality or an event of
ethnic significance, concern men whom the Hispanos have made their heroes.
<u>Corridos</u> are already circulating about the late United States Senator,
Dennis Chavez,[48] who died about two years ago. Governor Octaviano Larrazolo, who beat the best of the Anglo politicians in the early days of New
Mexico statehood, still lives in the folk songs and folk stories of his
people. On the other hand, some Hispanos who deceived or betrayed their
culture group are remembered only with bitterness and scorn often expressed
in "sayings" and in folk songs of the people. Folk songs of derision and
scorn are abundant to this day about the betrayal of the Hispanos by

---

[47]For a detailed description of this philanthropic, quasi-religious
fraternal organization see Josue Trujillo, <u>La Penitencia a Traves de la
Civilizacion</u> (Santa Fe: Santa Fe Press, 1957).

[48]An Hispano, for almost 30 years United States Senator from New
Mexico.

Governor Manuel Armijo, who, for a price, fled before the American Army
of conquest in 1846 and left his people and his land helpless and un-
defended before the onslaught of the Americans.

Cultural and racial groups are not wholly without organizations
that are powerful not only within the culture group, but also in the
outside political milieu. Among present-day Hispanos in New Mexico,
Colorado, California, and Arizona, such organizations as the Sociedad
Protectora Mutua de Trabajadores Unidos (SPMDTU),[49] the Alianza Hispano
Americana, and the League of United Latin American Citizens play important roles in both the political and social life of these people, and
have sometimes been used by political parties or political candidates to
further their own political aims and ambitions.[50]

Definition of the Situation and Reference Groups. Some of the
best known and most respected sociologists have been preoccupied with
the process of interaction of individuals. Simmel argued that the traditional concepts of social science such as "state," "church," etc., lacked "real"
social content and that it is only by studying the interactions between
individuals that the meaning of these concepts could be fully understood.
Durkheim makes the coercive aspect of the beliefs and practices which are
imposed upon the individual from without and to which he has to conform,

---

[49]A 50-year old organization of Hispano workers, with thousands
of members in several southwestern states.

[50]Hispano Republican leaders in Colorado made repeated efforts to
involve the SPMDTU in the recent Colorado gubernatorial and Denver mayoralty elections. Except for securing the political support of individual
officers and members of the organization, the politicians were firmly turned
down. However, all three have sometimes been separately captured politically at certain times in certain areas.

the central social fact of sociology. Max Weber defines the central social fact as the meaning which individuals in society attach to their own actions and those of others. Merton asserts that "definition of the situation" makes up the basic fact of social actions. Merton attempts to expand the conception of the "generalized other" of Herbert Mead into the concept of "reference group."

Reference group theory has much affinity with various concepts of "social frame of reference," "definition of the situation," and "patterns of expectations," since the reference group provides the source of interpretation and serves as a point of reference. Merton analyzes in detail several researches in The American Soldier,[51] showing multiple reference groups, which provide the contexts for evaluation by individuals.[52]

The concept of reference group has a distinctive place in the theoretical framework and theoretical orientation of this thesis and has an important bearing on the problems analyzed in this report, since it provides one of the foci on the structure and functions of the social environments in which individuals find themselves. Reference groups provide a frame of reference for attitude formation. Merton calls it a part of value-assimilation.

---

[51] Samuel Stouffer et al., The American Soldier: Adjustment During Army Life (Princeton University Press, 1949), I., Chap. VI.

[52] Robert K. Merton, Social Theory and Social Structure (Glencoe, Illinois: The Free Press, 1961), pp. 92-95.

As developed recently by Harold H. Kelley and Ralph Turner the
principal concept of reference group theory is that called "the comparison
type" which "provides a frame of comparison relative to which the individual evaluates himself and others."[53] Reference group as used in this
paper refers not only to groups, but also to social categories and has
specific application to the ethnic group under study.

Communication. It is now generally conceded that mass communication does not serve as a necessary and sufficient cause of audience
effects, but functions among and through a "nexus" of mediating factors
and influences, making mass communication a contributory agent but not
the sole cause in the process of reinforcing or changing attitudes and
opinions. For example, several studies show that people who change their
voting intentions do so as a result of personal contacts and not the influence of the newspapers or radio; there is a mediating or intervening
factor, usually the small group, intervening between the mass media and
the individual, modifying the effects of mass communication.[54] American
sociologists, at least, are now completely aware of the social context of
communication behavior. Merton sees opinion leaders as mediating between
the mass media and the individual. He sees media as being judged, censored,

---

[53]Harold H. Kelley, "Two Functions of Reference Groups," in G. E.
Swanson, T. M. Newcomb, and E. L. Hartley (eds.), Readings in Social
Psychology (New York: Henry Holt and Company, 1952), pp. 410-414;
Ralph H. Turner, "Role-taking, Role Standpoint, and Reference-group
Behavior," American Journal of Sociology, LVI (1956), 316-328.

[54]Paul F. Lazarsfeld, Bernard Berelson, and Hazel Gaudet, The
People's Choice (New York: Columbia University Press, 1955), Preface
xxiii.

and interpreted by the opinion leader within the group context. Merton's
studies have made the concept of the reference group, discussed above,
important in communication research.[55] Lazarsfeld's The People's Choice[56]
and Merton's[57] work on the role of opinion leaders in mass communication
appear to confirm the importance of personal influence in mass communication.

Although the various interviews in the panel survey included
questions regarding opinion leaders among the Hispanos in Denver and the
effect of personal contacts during the election campaign which took place
during the survey, the main question posed in this thesis has reference
to mass communication as it is siphoned through varying degrees or intensity of ethnicity and sees the ethnic population under study as an intervening factor intervening between the mass media and the individual as a
member of an ethnic group.

[55]Robert K. Merton, Social Theory and Social Structure (second
edition; New York: The Free Press, 1957) p. 52-53.

[56]Paul F. Lazarsfeld et al., op. cit., pp. 49-51.

[57]Robert K. Merton and Alice S. Kitt, "Contributions to the
Theory of Reference Group Behavior," in Robert K. Merton and Paul F.
Lazarsfeld (eds.), Continuities in Social Research (Glencoe, Illinois:
Free Press, 1950), pp. 40-109.

CHAPTER III

VOTING BEHAVIOR

The Concept

The research and findings of voting behavior in the last three
decades have definitely established that voting behavior is based not
on given election campaigns but on a gradual socialization which has
extended throughout the life of the voter. That most votes are not the
expression of "really fresh decisions" made during the political campaign and that it is the ultimate product of political socialization is
the most significant finding to come out of modern studies on voting
behavior.

A Review of the Literature

Contemporary sociological research about voting in the United
States has dealt mostly with how the individual voter decides to vote in
presidential elections. Most of these studies have been reports on the
formation of votes during presidential campaigns, that is, trying to
discover how and why people decide to vote as they do. Elections have
been analyzed by using official vote records to study the geographical
distribution of political expression in terms of votes cast for different candidates of different parties and political complexions. Some
have been ecological studies of voting, which examine vote records for
small units of a city or state in cases where there is considerable background data which are usually taken from census reports on racial composition, economic areas, etc., thus permitting some understanding of the
roles played by these factors in determining vote decisions.

Chronologically, the ecological analysis of voting was followed by the public opinion poll, which made possible the relating of political opinion and characteristics of the individual voter and permitted the study of the processes of decision-making in political behavior. Next came the "panel" method of interviewing, which permits tracing the development of a person's vote decision all through the political campaign and the election by repeated interviewing of the same person. By using this method, it is possible to analyze and discover both the predispositions and the stimuli to which he is subjected. The panel technique makes it possible to get at some important questions, such as: What is the effect of economic status upon vote? What role do radio, newspaper, and television play? How about the influence of family and friends? What and how do issues come into the picture?

Peter H. Rossi, in 1959, critically reviews the entire field of sociological research about American voting and finds that voting studies have produced a fair amount of knowledge of how a person's political preferences are shaped by his social class position, his religious affiliation, national origin, sex, and age.[1] But according to Philip H. Eunes, these studies have one common limitation: "The voter is cut off from his surroundings, suspended . . . above the political and social

---

[1]Peter H. Rossi, "Four Landmarks in Voting Research," in E. Burdick and A. J. Brodbeck (eds.), American Voting Behavior (New York: The Free Press, 1959), p. 84.

conditions of his community."[2] Eunes claims that political and social
community influences have been neglected. Studies in the fields of
political science and political history rarely attempt to assess empirically what the voters were thinking about or how they made up their
minds.

Leaving aside the few panel studies that have been made on voting
behavior, Eunes' criticism is well founded. Systematic research on voting has paralleled the more general empirical research movement, and it
is only recently that due consideration has been given to the fact that
voting is an individual act, and that it is essential that we have
information about individual persons.[3] This is true even in trying to

---

[2]Philip H. Eunes, "The Contextual Dimension in Voting" in William
N. McPhee and William A. Glaser (eds.), Public Opinion and Congressional
Elections (New York: The Macmillan Company, 1962), p. 180.

[3]The concept of the individual in society has been debated and
reflected upon for ages. Expressed in philosophical, ethical, and psychological terms, the social-individual relationship has been exten-
sively treated in the works of Kant, Marx, Tocqueville, and Freud.
The role of the individual in sociological analysis and in the
formulation of concepts of society by sociologists has had a checkered
existence. Some of the early sociologists tended to recognize the
importance of the individual in the individual-society combination, but
as sociology strived to establish itself as an independent discipline,
the importance of the individual as a factor in society was largely dis-
counted. The pendulum has now swung back to a point where the individual is becoming an important factor in sociological analysis.
Talcott Parsons puts forward a macro-functionalist theory of personality. He proposed linking the theories of Freud and Durkheim by
considering interaction as a system, contending this could correct both
Freud and Durkheim, since, according to Parsons, Freud failed to consider the fact that the individual's interaction with others forms a
system and Durkheim failed to see that social systems consist in the
interaction of the personalities. Parsons contends that, basically, the
structure of the social system is rooted in the concrete human individual

guage the relation to behavior of sociological factors, for although it
is sometimes possible to make inferences about individual behavior from
what is known about group behavior, often group behavior cannot be fully
understood except in terms of the behavior of individuals in that group.

Developments in the field of group dynamics are indicative of
the growing recognition of the role of the individual. This, of course,
ties in with the increasing awareness that too often, in sociological
research and analysis, the individual has been neglected.

There is now a definite movement which seeks to overcome the
difficulties of aggregate analysis by developing methods that yield data
about individual people. But the true possibilities of the interview
survey in voting research and as a means of getting data about individual
people developed as a result of the work of Lazarsfeld, Berelson, and
Guadet in Erie County, Ohio in 1940.[4] For the first time the role of
interpersonal influence was recognized in shaping and reinforcing political opinion within primary groups defined by the social structure of
the local community. The same technique was used in the 1948 election
in Elmira, New York.[5] In 1944, the National Opinion Research Center

---

as a physical organism acting in a physical environment and that the
individuals as personalities participate in the process of social interaction through various roles.

[4]Lazarsfeld, et al., op. cit., Preface, x.

[5]Bernard R. Berelson, Paul F. Lazarsfeld, and William N. McPhee,
Voting (Chicago: University of Chicago Press, 1954), p. 103.

conducted the first nationwide study using the sample survey with the
distinguishing characteristic of the interview-reinterview design.[6] In
1952, the Survey Research Center made an even more extensive study but
with greater emphasis on attitudinal variables and more of a psychological than a sociological orientation.[7] In 1956, the same research center
duplicated the 1952 study, but instead of emphasizing a single class of
factors, it shifts emphasis to less immediate or direct factors or
influences. The future of research in voting behavior points to a merg-
ing of sociological and psychological factors, theoretical orientation,
and analysis. The framework for full-scale systematic theory and
research must be adequate to deal with the very complex nature of voting
behavior.

Election studies have rarely dealt with voting as a key mechanism
of consensus. Considered from this point of view, various categories of
voters are not only deviants from majority patterns, but necessary for
the maintenance of the political system. Stability in a democracy
requires that all major political parties include adherents from all
divisions of the population. Members of minority groups are often nomi-
nated by political parties in order to have leaders from diverse groups
and also to represent symbolically the party's concern with these
groups. Another problem studied in recent voting research is that of

---

[6]No published report of this study is yet available.

[7]See Angus Campbell, Gerald Gurin, and Warren E. Miller, The
.Voter Decides (Evanston: Row, Peterson and Company, 1954).

agreement on issues across group lines and party cleavages resulting from
multi-group affiliations or loyalties.[8]

One of the most encouraging trends is emerging in the work of such
men as Lipset, Blau, Lazarsfeld, Davis, and McPhee, who are giving greater
consideration in the analysis and understanding of voting behavior to
what has variably been called "community context," "structural context,"
and "structural effects." All these terms are used to designate a generic
class of social influences upon individual behavior and attitudes, although
they sometimes refer to the more limited idea of direct interaction among
individuals.[9]

In perhaps over-simplified terms, these are pioneer efforts to
define and measure more precisely the conditions under which known influences operate in the act of voting. There are different kinds of community contexts, such as demographic structure, party preponderance, and
local climates of opinion.

Voting behavior is grounded in the whole history and present situation of the individual. The prime variables in determining voting preferences include: the economic status of the individual, religion, place
of residence, education, chronological age, sex, nationality, previous
voting record, voting preference of cue-giving individuals and groups,

[8]Berelson, et al., op. cit., pp. 185-212.

[9]William N. McPhee and William A. Glaser (eds.), Public Opinion
and Congressional Elections (New York: The Free Press of Glencoe, The
Macmillan Company, 1962), pp. 180-210.

membership in formal organizations, and the character of opposing candidates
and issues. But there are other important factors governing the general
environmental context of the individual, such as war, or those influencing his immediate circumstances, such as personally knowing a candidate,
having received a favor from the candidate or his party, and so on.

To explain why people vote as they do, there have been accumulated
not only poll data, but statistically worked-out relations between voting
behavior and economic and other indexes, intensive interviewing surveys,
historical analyses, and case studies of single elections. Louis H. Bean
has been able to establish relationships between the percentage of the
vote received by political candidates and fluctuations in other phenomenon.[10] In Texas, for instance, a few counties went Republican in 1940;
in counties in which 3 to 10 per cent of the population was of German
background, the shift to the Republicans was 3 to 10 percentage points
over the 1936 figures; in counties where 15 to 20 percent of the population
was of German origin, the increase was 24 to 48 percentage points in the
Republican vote.[11] An explanation for this difference was found to rest
upon the Roosevelt record in international relations and the Wilkie German
nationality origin.

Other analyses have related voting choice to average rentals, re-

---

[10]Louis H. Bean, How to Predict Elections (New York: Alfred A.
Knopf, Inc., 1948).

[11]Norman John Powell, Anatomy of Public Opinion (Englewood Cliffs,
New Jersey: Prentice-Hall, Inc., 1951), p. 515.

ligious composition of the community and exposure to different types and intensity of mass media communication. The overall result has been the belief that people's votes are much more nearly the outcome of continuing and permanent factors than of transient variables of a particular occasion and candidate. Data from more recent studies indicate that it is the characteristics of the voter rather than those of the candidates that determine the voter's choice at election time. Hadley Cantril points out that older people tend to vote Republican more than young people; those in the upper income group tend to vote Republican more than those in the lowest income group by about 2 to 1; and so on.[12]

Although political propaganda is of some value in influencing voting behavior, most people make their voting choices even before any campaigns. As has been pointed out, significant correlations exist between the individual's background and his political selection. What happens is that people tend to expose themselves only to the propaganda of the group they support and undecided voters avoid propaganda exposure. But propaganda serves to activate voters' political predispositions which, in turn, are mostly based on economic, historical, and nationality background. An analysis by Lazarsfeld, Berelson and Gaudet points to the fact that personal contact seems to be the best way to change voting anticipations although mass propaganda, too, has its effects.[13] For example, in an

---

[12]Hadley Cantril, "The Intensity of an Attitude," *Journal of Abnormal and Social Psychology*, 1946, XLIV, pp. 129-135.

[13]Lazarsfeld, *et al.*, *op. cit.*, pp. 137-148.

analysis of a 1945 municipal election in Detroit, Carl O. Smith and
Stephen O. Sarasohn show that propaganda did influence people to vote
and, also, determined thousands of voters. The propaganda used was of
an inflammatory nature; neighborhood weekly newspapers charged that one
of the candidates wanted to open white neighborhoods to Negro residents;
Poles and other groups were told that the value of their homes would drop
when the Negroes moved in. At the same time, this same candidate's opposition distributed leaflets to Negro homes which declared that the
candidate was an enemy of the Negro. What happened is best exemplified
by what took place in Polish neighborhoods. The candidate opposing the
candidate charged with wanting to flood white neighborhoods with Negroes
had received only 17 per cent of the primary vote in these districts, but
he received 39 per cent of the vote in the general election.[14]

The close link between political behavior patterns and religious
beliefs and practices has been established many times in a variety of
studies.[15] In their book, Voting, Bernard R. Berelson, Paul F. Lazarsfeld,
and William N. McPhee, state, "In contemporary America, political events
and social differentiation have combined to produce three major types of
political cleavage: (1) occupational, income, and status cleavages,
(2) religious, racial, and ethnic cleavages, and (3) regional and urban-

[14]Carl O. Smith and Stephen O. Sarasohn, "Hate Propaganda in Detroit"
Public Opinion Quarterly; X, 1946; pp. 24-52.

[15]Seymour Martin Lipset, Political Man (Garden City, New York:
Doubleday and Company, Inc., 1960), pp. 244-248.

rural cleavages."[16] Lazarsfeld, Berelson, and Hazel Gaudet repeatedly
found in their studies of voting behavior in Erie County, Ohio, in 1940,
that people vote "in groups."[17]

Some studies of the relationship between religion and support of
extremist or democratic political parties are revealing. French and
Italian Catholic workers may vote for conservative parties because their
Catholicism was stronger than their resentments about their class status.[18]
Other studies have shown that religion affected support of the Nazi more
than any other factor. The Nazi main voting strength was in Protestant
small communities and weakest in Catholic regions and cities.[19]

Hispano workers in the United States Southwest, often in the past
and at times today, vote against their own interests because of church
opposition. In early New Mexico, Hispanos repeatedly defeated attempts
to establish public schools because of active opposition on the part of
the Catholic Church.[20] Catholic Church opposition to such measures as

---

[16]Berelson, et al., op. cit., pp. 185-212.

[17]Paul F. Lazarsfeld, Bernard Berelson, and Hazel Gaudet, The
People's Choice (New York: Columbia University Press, 1948), pp. 137-148;
also Daniel T. Valdes, "Religious Preference and Voting Behavior in Denver
in the 1960 Presidential Election," unpublished term paper, 1961.

[18]Seymour Martin Lipset, Political Man (Garden City, New York;
Doubleday and Company, Inc., 1960), pp. 100-101.

[19]Ibid., p. 146.

[20]In 1855 some legislators, attempting to enact laws for the estab-
lishment and administration of public schools and imposing taxes for
their support, found the opposition so bitter on the part of Hispano

federal aid to education and birth control has sometimes caused Hispanos
to vote against office seekers who are known to favor such measures.

In this research project the composition and structuring of religious-ethnic groupings is studied with the emphasis on the relationship
between traditional orientation (religious-ethnic affiliation, and identification) and voting behavior among American Hispanos, and how this in
turn is influenced by class-economic interests and system-integrating
processes (mass communication, etc.). Granted the findings of ethnic
consciousness, is it translated into political (more precisely, voting)
behavior corresponding to the degree of ethnic consciousness expressed
or objectively determined?

---

representatives from Taos, Rio Arriba, Santa Ana, and Socorro Counties
that a sufficient vote for passage of the measures could not be secured
except by exempting these counties from the provisions of the acts.   It
was, therefore, decided that a vote be taken in these counties to let
the people decide whether to come within the provisions of the acts.
Of 5,053 who voted, only 37 were in favor of the school provisions.

CHAPTER IV

THE HISTORICAL PROCESS OF CHANGING RELATIONS

Interaction as Part of a Continuous Process of Change

As has already been pointed out, interaction between ethnic and racial groups is a part of a continuous process of change, maintained within both stable and changing social structures. Three aspects of this process of change affecting dominant-minority relations have been identified and analyzed by sociologists. They are the historical process of changing mutual relations, the contemporary processes of stable interaction, and the characteristic processes of interaction in time of stress.

E. Franklin Frazier has developed a scheme for the analysis of the historical processes of relationships in which he stresses the importance of initial contact between different groups and the stages through which this initial contact develops in the ecological, economic and political contexts. For example, trade and barter between diverse racial, ethnic or cultural groups may lead to conficts which may eventually lead to dominance of one group over the other or the substitution of one type of dominance for an old one.[1]

Historical Factors in Sociological Analysis

As long as man has existed, some human beings have had dominance over others. In the last four hundred years, this dominance has been based on and characterized by "race consciousness." Europeans discovered,

---

[1] E. Franklin Frazier, Race and Culture Contacts in the Modern World (New York: Alfred A. Knopf, Inc., 1957), Chapter 13.

colonized, and established hegemony over other peoples. This was true of
Frenchmen, Englishmen, Spaniards, and other Europeans as they established
dominance over the colored peoples of Africa and the Western Hemisphere.
In the American Southwest, the Spaniard conquered the Indian and was in
turn conquered by the Anglo.

What happened in the United States Southwest and the present relations of the Anglo and the Hispano in this part of the world is explain-
able in large measure by forces present in its own history, although complete
understanding can be reached only by viewing this situation as part of a
larger historical process, such as dominant-minority relations, which have
arisen in modern times as a result of political annexation, colonialism,
slavery, and immigration. It is necessary to place emphasis on the fact
that all dominant-minority relations occur within a given society and its
particular social system; and both society and its particular social systems
must be understood within their historical context. In spite of the current
negative attitude toward history and ethnology by some sociologists, knowledge of, and consideration for, the historical background of the problems
they study will always remain a necessary part of any sociological study.

Opposition which arises between two peoples living in the same area
is a historical fact, as it is sociologically natural. The degree and the
form which this opposition takes is important to the understanding of any
current relations between two groups. To an important extent, the preval-
ence of ethnic antagonism between the Hispano and the Anglo is due to the
unique historical circumstance which created the dominant-minority situation
in the American Southwest.

Historical Political Roles and Behavior of the Hispano

Even to this day, there does not exist a comprehensive and analytical study of the historical evolution of politics in the American Southwest in the Hispanic states of Colorado, New Mexico, Texas, and California.
The writer has been unable to find any interpretative studies of political
developments, institutions, or events in these states which give proper
recognition, or even consideration, to the political cleavages and constant
efforts toward consensus which have existed for one hundred years between
the two dominant cultures in these states, the Anglo and the Hispanic.

The history of the politics of these states is the history of
government and of man's relation to man dating back to two hundred years
of government rule under the Spanish, followed by twenty-five years under
the Republic of Mexico, the coming of the Americans in 1846, and reaching
into the present era. The story of Spanish exploration, colonization,
and rule has already been told in innumerable books, articles, and pamph-
lets with varying degrees of truthfulness, exaggeration, misrepresentation,
and thoroughness. But as Carey McWilliams points out in his enlightening
book, North from Mexico, "The romantic, heroic side has been accepted and
enshrined; the prosaic or mundane phase has been ignored or discredited."[2]

Studies dealing with the period since the American occupation are
rich and abundant, dealing with every phase of life in this state since
the coming of the Americans. But never has an attempt been made to write
a detailed, comprehensive political history. Nor has there been, for that

_____

[2]Carey McWilliams, North from Mexico (Philadelphia and New York:
J. B. Lippincott Company, 1949), p. 19.

matter, any detailed and analytical reports on the historical evolution
of politics or a really comprehensive study of historical and present-day
political developments, events, and institutions.

The patron system. The most significant single political and economic fact is much of the southwest for nearly two centuries (1680-1880)
was the existence of the patron system. A New World transmutation of the
feudal system of the old, the patron system was one of the major influences
in the shaping and development of the politics of this area. The patron
system was both the personal and institutional authority of the rico over
his laborers. It had as its basis the economic and social relationship
between the big land owner and sheep baron, the pobre with insufficient
resources to provide the minimum necessities of life, the debtor-peon,
who had the misfortune of falling into debt to the rico, and the captive
Indian slaves. The patron system was a variation of the plantation system
of the South. The ricos were the plantation owners, the Indians were the
slaves, and the peones, the "poor White trash." In some respects, the
patron system was an institution recognized by law, but economic conditions
fathered and nurtured it. The system was based on three separate and distinct degrees or conditions of servitude, personified by the debtor-peon,
the captive Indian slave, and the farmer-peon relationships.

In 1780, which is the mid-point of the period between the reconquest
of New Mexico by DeVargas in 1692 and the American occupation in 1846,

there were approximately 40,000 Spanish people in the territory now com-
prising the states of Colorado and New Mexico. It is impossible to
estimate accurately the number belonging to each of the distinct classes
which made up the White population in the province during Spanish and
Mexican rule. A rough estimate based on the population figures in the
year 1780 and its geographical distribution, plus certain specific economic data, indicates the following population components:[3] The depend-

Ricos	110	families
Debtor-Peones	2,500	"
Farmer-Peones	12,000	"
Paisanos	25,000	"
Military	400	"

ency of the peon (a word still used among the Hispano to designate a
ranch or common laborer) on the patron created the patron-peon relationship by which the patron controlled the votes of his peones. This in
turn established what has become known as the patron system in politics.
With the coming of the Americans, the patron became the instrument
through which the sizable block of peon votes was controlled for the new
Anglo leaders.

From Santa Fe north to the present Colorado border and beyond, a
different class of people made up the bulk of the population. During
the 17th and 18th centuries soldiers, artisans, and workers of the Spanish peasant class, as well as less favored colonists, were given smaller
individual grants of land or in some cases larger grants to groups

---

[3] Pedro Bautista Pino, Exposicion Sucinta y Sencilla de la Provincia de Nuevo Mexico (Mexico City: Imprenta de Lara, 1849).

composed of several families, known as community land grants.[4] Most
frequently, each family received a comparatively small tract of fertile
land along the rivers and streams in addition to timber and grazing
lands held on a community basis. These less-favored colonists made
their homes in the rugged, narrow valleys of the Rio Arriba country and
became America's true and only peasants known to this day as paisanos,
"men of the country." They were rugged, individualistic men of the
soil, fiercely proud and determinedly independent, and so they remain to
this day, except for the thousands who have become part farmers, part
migratory workers, those who depend on state, county, or local jobs for
a living, and many more thousands of their descendents who make up the
bulk of the present-day Hispano population in Colorado and New Mexico.

Experience in local self-government. The Hispano had experience
in local self-government comparable to that of the Anglo settlers on the
East Coast. From the beginning, as in the English Colonies, the Spanish
citizens of any villa or town elected a cabildo or town council which
had combined legislative, executive, and judicial powers in local
affairs. Otherwise, all power was vested in an appointive governor, who
in turn appointed all subordinate officials. This was also the system
in effect in the English Colonies until the Declaration of Independence
in 1776.

----

[4]R. E. Twitchell, Leading Facts of New Mexico History (Cedar
Rapids, Iowa: The Torch Press, 1911), p. 107.

The Mexican Declaration of Independence was proclaimed in 1822,
and thereafter the Mexicans enjoyed a fuller measure of popular government, similar in many respects to the republican form of government in
effect in the original thirteen colonies subsequent to 1776.[5] There was
also an elected provincial council or legislative assembly. This legislative body held its sessions at Durango, Mexico and was composed of
delegates from each of the provinces.[6]

The Hispano's eager response to all sorts of demagoguery and his
marked tendency to follow the dictates of machine politics, or more
accurately stated, the facility with which the Hispano has been made a
victim and tool of machine politics, is simply and principally due to
economic and sociological reasons. His poverty and his historical
dependence on the rich for leadership have been the Hispano's primary
political weaknesses. The nature of the family unit among the Hispanos,
the kinship among nearly all the families in a given political subdivi-
sion, as well as the Hispano's dependence on a feudal relationship to
some leader were tailor-made for machine politics. These conditions
have also resulted in a personalism in government similar to that in
many Latin American countries where identical conditions prevailed.
There has been among the Hispanos loyalty to individuals instead of to

---

[5] Even before the Spanish Colonies in North America won their
independence from Spain, there were at least 14 elected town councils in
New Mexico, being found in all towns with a population of 1,000 or over.

[6] Le Baron B. Prince, A Concise History of New Mexico (Cedar
Rapids, Iowa: The Torch Press, 1914), p. 111.

ideas. Instead of "prohibitionists," "states righters," and "federal-
ists," Hispanos have had their "Chavezistas," ad infinitum.

The Anglos in these areas have made their influence in government
felt through instrumentalities of their economic or social interests
such as the cattle growers associations, the state medical societies,
taxpayers associations, educational associations, labor organizations,
etc. The Hispanos as a group have channelled their strength through
political leaders.

The role of the Catholic Church and its representatives played in
the government and politics of New Mexico and Colorado must be considered in relation to the fact that for 250 years there was no separation
of church and state as we know it today. As a result, there was never a
clearly established and defined boundary between civil-military and
church authority, privileges and obligations. This naturally brought
about almost constant strife between the state and the church throughout
Spanish rule.

There were quarrels about ecclesiastical privileges and immuni-
ties, the extent of religious jurisdiction and censures, Indian labor,
and control and direction of the missions. The religious authorities
charged the civil government had "turned the convents into trading posts
and had made the friars its hucksters."[7] These charges were countered

_____

[7] r. V. Scholes, "State and Church in New Mexico," VII, _Publica-
tions in History_ (Santa Fe: Historical Society of New Mexico, 1937).

by charges by civil authorities that the friars were neglecting their
duties. All during the Spanish rule in New Mexico, the clergy was con-
sulted regarding purely civil questions, and it frequently participated
in the formulation of government policies. Several priests became more
active politically after the American Government was established. Seven
of the members of the first New Mexico legislature under American rule
were priests, and Father Antonio Jose Martinez was elected president of
the council at the first session. Father Jose Manuel Gallegos was the
first delegate from New Mexico to the United States Congress.[8]

The Anglo-American conquest and the territorial government. On
August 18, 1846 Kearney entered Santa Fe. The following are excerpts
from the speech General Kearney delivered as Conqueror of New Mexico:
" . . . We do not mean to murder or rob you of your property . . . You
are not longer Mexican subjects; you are now become American citizens
. . . I do hereby proclaim my intention to establish in this Department
a civil government, on a republican basis, similar to those of our own
states. General Armijo has fled . . . I am now your Governor.[9] When
General Kearney organized the new government, both Anglo-Americans and
the new Americans[10] were represented. In the new government the natives

---

[8] T. C. Donnelly, Government of New Mexico (Albuquerque: University of New Mexico Press, 1947), p. 19.

[9] Le Baron B. Prince, op. cit., p. 111.

[10] Mexicans who automatically became American citizens under terms
of the Treaty of Guadalupe Hidalgo.

were quick to curry favor with the new rulers.

A new territorial government went into operation on March 3, 1851.
Thus began almost three quarters of a century of territorial rule for
New Mexico during which the people were not allowed to elect their own
governor or other state officials, the governor being appointed by the
president with the consent of the Senate, and the governor in turn appoint-
ing all other state officials. As a result the politics of the territory,
although having a flavor all their own, were greatly influenced by
national politics during this "trying out" period. Not until 1912 was
the territory elevated to statehood. At the time of the American Conquest
there were 60,000 Spanish-speaking people living in New Mexico and only
about five hundred Anglo-Americans.[11]

When New Mexico became a territory, the Republicans were in power
in Washington. This is one of the major reasons why the majority of the
Hispanos were registered as Republicans until the Roosevelt New Deal era
of 1932. Since statehood (1912) two Hispanos had been elected to the
governorship in New Mexico, but only one, Octaviano Larrazolo, served his
full term.

In summary, the sixty-odd years of territorial status saw a struggle by the Hispanos to assert themselves in a government set up to give

---

[11]Between 1845 and 1912, southern Colorado was a part of the New
Mexico Territory, so from this point on, the historical background refers
specifically to New Mexico and Colorado, since the study is directed
primarily toward these two areas.

them only a measure of self-government. The Hispanos held nominal control of a comparatively impotent assembly and elected delegates to a
national congress where they had no vote. The Anglo-Americans always
maintained control of the courts. Even after statehood and to this day,
of twenty-three supreme court justices, only one has been an Hispano.

The Hispanos received token recognition in state appointive
posts during the territorial period. In the first assembly in 1847, not
a single Anglo was elected to the territorial council (senate) and only
four (of twenty-one members) to the house. As late as 1882, thirty
years after the conquest, only four Anglos were serving on the legislative council and four in the house.

The number of offices held by the Hispanos as compared to those
held by the Anglos throughout the territorial period (1847-1912) is
shown on Table II. The table shows that of 256 top officials appointed
to rule over the people of New Mexico for over sixty years, only 28 were
Hispanos. This same pattern of token representation was followed in the
appointment of territorial boards. Such boards as the Territorial Board
of Equalization, the New Mexico Board of Health, the Territorial Board
of Education, and various institutional boards, were all appointed by non-
elected governors. Of nearly 150 members appointed to such boards, only
15 were Hispanos, a repetition of the 10 to 1 ratio found in favor of the
Anglos throughout the territorial period.

Hispanos under statehood. Since statehood, the Hispanos had

TABLE II

NEW MEXICO TERRITORIAL OFFICERS

Offices	Anglo Americans	Hispano Americans	Mixed
Governors	18	None	1
Secretaries of State	20	1	
Attorneys General	26	None	
Auditors	18	9	
Treasurers	18	1	
Adjutants General	18	1	
Penitentiary Superintendents	6	1	
Chief Justices (of Supreme Court)	16	None	
U. S. Attorneys (in New Mexico)	19	None	
Collectors of Internal Revenue	9	None	
Superintendents of Public Instruction	1	5	
District Judges	59	1	
Delegates in Congress (Elected)	9	10	
Totals	229	35	1

Source: New Mexico Archives, Historical Documents of New
Mexico.

until the 1950 setback, improved their representation in government in spite of the rapid increase in the Anglo population. At the time of the American conquest, Anglos represented less than ten per cent of the White population. By 1900 they represented about one-third of the population. In 1930 the ratio was 60-40 in favor of the Hispano, but by 1940, it was 50-50, and today the Anglos constitute at least 60 per cent of the population. Since statehood, an average of two Hispanos have been elected in each administration to high elective state posts. Of the 11 different men who have served as United States Senators, only two have been Hispanos, and of 13 congressmen, five have belonged to this cultural group.

Political parties, defined as clearly recognized groups of citizens banded together for the attainment of announced political objectives (employing party machinery such as rallies, internal organization, etc.), did not exist in New Mexico prior to the American conquest. It is fairly certain that political parties, labeled by name on voting ballots, were unknown in New Mexico until they were introduced by the Anglo Americans.

It was several years after New Mexico was conquered by the Americans that the first political parties appeared, although the Anglos and Hispano collaborators were already politically aligned against the majority of the population and the real leaders of the Hispano-Americans. One-time Governor of New Mexico, Miguel Antonio Otero, Jr., states in his book, My Life on the Frontier, "The Otero, Armijo, and Chaves fami-

lies were all for the American Party as against the Mexican Party."[12]
This was apparently in the early 1850's when there was already crystal-
ization of unity of the conquerors and the collaborators on the one hand,
and the conquered people on the other. Parties, as Otero calls them,
were not formally organized parties.

To understand properly New Mexico politics and its political
parties during the territorial period (1850-1912), it is necessary to
state briefly the origin and development of the political parties
nationally and to establish the period of dominance of each of the parties. By 1832 the Democratic Party as we know it today had taken definite form. It had been organized by Andrew Jackson and others who had
broken away from the old Republican Party. Those remaining in the Republican Party called themselves National Republicans. Two years later
the National Republicans, grouping themselves with other factions, organized the Whig Party. For twenty years (1834-1854), crucial years for
New Mexico, the two dominant parties were the Democratic Party and the
Whig Party. In 1854, as a result of the increasing seriousness of the
slavery question, the Republican Party as we know it today came into
existence, and the Democratic and Republican Parties have continued
down to our day as the two dominant parties. Of the fifteen presidents
who served during the sixty years of New Mexico Territorial Government,
twelve were Republicans. Table III graphically illustrates in two and

---

[12]Miguel A. Otero, My Life on the Frontier (Albuquerque:
University of New Mexico Press, 1937), p. 138.

TABLE III

67

CAPSULE ANALYSIS OF ONE HUNDRED YEARS
OF NEW MEXICO POLITICS

Terr. Period	Governor	Assembly	Del. to Cong.	Major Political Characteristics
1850-51	Whig			Anglo versus Hispano
1852-53	Dem.			
1854-55	Dem.			
1856-57	Dem.		Rep.	Rule by Southerners, continuation of
1859-59	Dem.		Rep.	Anglo-Hispano conflict
1860-61	Rep.		Rep.	
1862-63	Rep.		Rep.	United States Civil War
1864-65	Rep.		Dem.	
1866-69	Rep.		Rep.	Domination of territorial politics
1870-83	Rep.		Rep.	by the "Santa Fe Ring."
1884-85	Dem.	Rep.	Dem.	Strife and turmoil, Rump assembly
1886-87	Rep.	Rep.	Dem.	Bar Association domination of assem-
1888-89	Rep.	Rep.	Dem.	bly, rise of Republican machine rule.
1890-91	Rep.	Rep.	Dem.	
1892-93	Dem.	Rep.	Dem.	
1894-95	Dem.	Rep.	Rep.	
1896-1911	Rep.	Rep.	Rep.	"Otero" rule, height of Republican machine politics
State-hood	Gov.	St. Leg.	U.S. Cong.	. . . . . STATEHOOD, 1912
1912-19	Dem.	Rep.	Dem.	Revival of the "Catronites" and
1920-23	Dem.	Rep.	Dem.	Republican rule, locally. Teapot
1924-27	Dem.	Rep.	Dem.	Dome scandal.
1928-31	Rep.	Rep.	Rep.	
1932-35	Dem.	Rep.	Dem.	
1936-39	Dem.	Dem.	Dem.	The great depression, The New Deal;
1940-43	Dem.	Dem.	Dem.	mass switch of Hispano voters to
1944-47	Dem.	Dem.	Dem.	Democratic Party; rising influence of
1948-50	Dem.	Dem.	Dem.	"Little Texas."
1950-53	Rep.	Dem.	Dem.	
1954-56	Dem.	Dem.	Dem.	Peace and prosperity; almost complete
1956-58	Rep.	Dem.	Dem.	control of state politics by Anglo-
1959-60	Dem.	Dem.	Dem.	Americans

four-year sequences, periods of dominance in New Mexico politics of the
two major parties.

Since the coming of the Americans to the United States Southwest, there have been two dominant, and in some instances conflicting,
cultures: the Spanish or Hispano and the Anglo or American. This conflict of cultures has repeatedly projected itself into politics.

Both political parties have been scrupulously trying to avoid
"racial" conflicts in the consideration and enactment of state legisla-
tion, but in some notable instances, "racial" alignments in the legislature have affected the course of New Mexico legislative history. In
1926, such an alignment occurred in the consideration of an election
code. The proposed bill called for the denial of assistance in marking
a ballot to any person unless he made an affidavit that he was blind or
could not read either English or Spanish. Perhaps a good thing in itself, but it was aimed primarily at discouraging Hispanos from voting,
since illiteracy among the Hispanos has always been greater than among
the Anglos. Of the twenty to twenty-five thousand voters who were il-
literate in 1926, probably fifteen to twenty thousand were Hispanos.
Consequently, the Hispanos in the legislature united solidly in opposition, and the proposed election code was killed in committee. Later
Hispanos were responsible for the defeat of many of the legislators who
supported the measure in the legislature. Senator Bronson Cutting
vigorously opposed the bill, and won an almost unprecedented support of
of the Hispano voters.

In the 1935 session of the legislature, a bill providing for a direct primary was introduced but defeated 34 to 13 with Anglo machine politicians lining up with the almost solid opposition of Hispano legislators to effect the defeat. The direct primary was a step toward fuller democratic government, but here again it was aimed at the Hispano minority, which under the convention system could still bargain for power.

The most dramatic "racial" alignment in the history of the New Mexico legislature occurred during the 1949 legislative session.[13] In the consideration of a fair employment practices act designed to abolish discrimination in employment, the Anglos were almost solidly lined up against the measure; nearly all the Hispano legislators and a few Anglo legislators from Spanish speaking districts were united in support of the measure. The political machine was caught between the two groups. It secretly instructed its Hispano and Anglo legislative leaders to take every step to prevent the measure from coming out of committee. The political machine wanted to avoid any showdown on the floor of the senate and house of representatives. Two Hispanos, former House Majority Floor Leader Fidel Gonzales of Las Vegas, and the erstwhile political machine leader, Victor Salazar of Albuquerque, made strenuous but futile efforts to keep the bill bottled up in committee. Taking the initiative away from the machine politicians, Sixto Leyba and five other Hispano

[13]The writer as State Chairman of the New Mexico Human Relations Council, led the struggle for FEPC enactment and was a witness to these events.

legislators forced it out of committee in the house of representatives, the bill already having been passed in the senate under the expert guidance of then State Senator Tibo Chavez. When the bill came up for a vote in the house in the closing hours of the legislative session, the bill passed 25-24, on a strictly geographic and cultural vote, with not a single Hispano voting against it.

The 1949 legislature provided still another case of "racial" alignment on the part of New Mexico legislators. The reapportionment bills providing for a reapportionment of legislators, although justifiable because of pronounced shifts and increases in population in the state, would have further decreased the number of Hispano representatives and senators. The various bills proposing reapportionment of legislators on a straight population basis were all killed in committees by the almost solid opposition of Hispano legislators. A watered-down compromise bill finally did become law, with still a substantial number of Hispano legislators voting against its passage. The Hispanos had good reason to fear a further loss of power and prestige in the New Mexico legislative bodies. By 1949 the number of Hispano legislators had hit an almost record low, as indicated in Figure 1, which illustrates graphically the number of Hispano legislators compared to the number of Anglo legislators from 1913 to 1960.

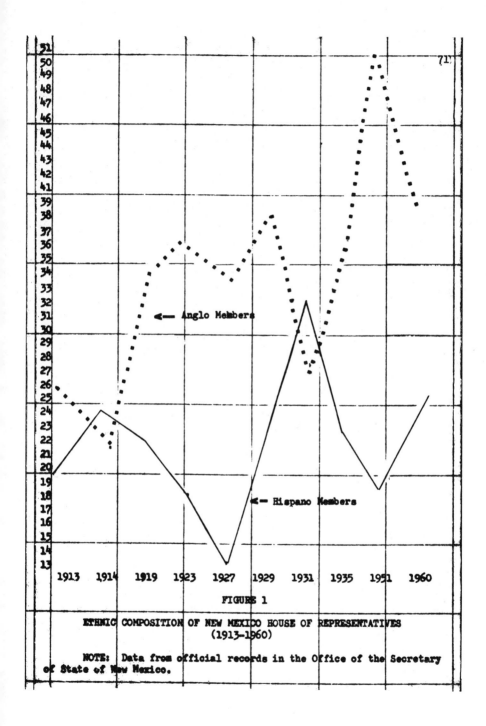

FIGURE 1

ETHNIC COMPOSITION OF NEW MEXICO HOUSE OF REPRESENTATIVES
(1913-1960)

NOTE: Data from official records in the Office of the Secretary of State of New Mexico.

CHAPTER V

THE CONTEMPORARY PROCESS
OF POLITICAL INTERACTION

The political role, status, and behavior of the Hispano
in the United States Southwest in the 20th Century until the end
of World War II (1946) had a checkered existence. Sometimes
sporadic attempts to secure important seats at the table of
political power had been successful but only in very few instances
and areas.[1] On the whole, the three million Hispanos in these
states have been a submerged, frustrated, apathetic, and un-
organized citizen group, without leaders selflessly devoted
to the causes which would benefit Hispanos. There has been
anger and disappointment among the young and hopelessness among
the elders.

Whereas the Anglo frequently refuses to vote for an
Hispano candidate for office, the Hispano has almost always
voted strictly along party lines, with little or no thought as
to the cultural background of the candidates. "I'd rather not
vote than vote for a 'Mexican!'" is a phrase often attributed to
the Anglo citizens of the United States Southwest. This phrase
was heard often by the writer when campaigning for U. S. Senator
Dennis Chavez in 1948.

---

[1]Not even spotty success in establishing their political
identity and importance had characterized the half-hearted and badly
organized efforts of Hispanos in California, Texas, or Arizona.
Only at the local level in Colorado and on both state and local
levels in New Mexico had there been partial and sporadic success
in politics. In Colorado, Conejos, and Huerfano Counties, after
nearly 30 years of Anglo domination in these predominantly Hispano
counties, the Hispanos now have regained control of county
governments. In New Mexico, Hispanos at times have successfully
repulsed efforts of the increasing Anglo (southern oriented) population to take two congressional seats from the Hispanos.

The Hispano Political Status in New Mexico

Election returns indicate that a substantial number of south-
eastern Anglos of New Mexico will not vote for an Hispano.[2] In the
1950 primary election, in Chavez County, a total of about six thousand
votes were cast in the Democratic gubernatorial primary race. David
Chavez, the only Spanish speaking candidate in this race, received a
mere 485 votes. Of 5,500 votes cast in Lea County, Mr. Chavez received
only 220 votes, or four per cent of the votes polled in the county.
Not so many, but still a substantial number of eastern New Mexico Anglos,
would rather cross party lines than vote for an Hispano candidate, as
indicated in Table IV. A much smaller number of Hispanos will desert
their party to express preference for a candidate of their own cultural
background. Table V indicates that where party loyalty is involved,
they vote according to party, except in elections highly charged with
ethnic implications.[3]

Greater political independence and a greater ethnic conscious-

---

[2]Analyses of election returns in southern Colorado where there
are often Hispano candidates for public office, also show the same ten-
dency. On a state-wide basis, election returns in 1958 when Charles S.
Vigil, former United States Attorney for Colorado ran for Colorado State
Attorney General, the same tendency can be seen. Vigil was the only
Democratic candidate for a major state office defeated in the election.

[3]This was shown in the Santa Fe School Board election in 1956.
Since 1912, Anglos held a majority on the school board. For several
years, "anti-Mejicanismo" had been charged against school administrators.
Hispanos called mass meetings and decided to run Hispano, non-partisan
candidates, and elected all of them.

TABLE IV

VOTES CAST IN 1950 GENERAL ELECTION SHOWING
AN ANGLO VOTING BEHAVIOR PATTERN*

Anglo Counties	For Attorney General (Anglo Rep. versus Hispano Dem.)			For St. Treasurer (Both candidates Anglo)		No. Voting for Anglo Dem. but not for Hispano Dem.
	Anglo Rep.	Hispano Dem.		Anglo Rep.	Anglo Dem.	
Eddy	3560	3560		2784	4337	777
Colfax	2967	3010		2398	3470	460
Curry	2481	3590		2010	4099	509
Dona Ana	4667	4375		3763	4716	341
Lea	1559	2671		1064	3226	555

Total voting in five counties for
Anglo Democrats, but not for the
Hispano Democrat running against
an Anglo Republican 2642

*New Mexico Blue Book, 1952, published by New Mexico Secretary of
State, Santa Fe, New Mexico.

TABLE V

VOTES CAST IN 1950 GENERAL ELECTION SHOWING
AN HISPANO VOTING BEHAVIOR PATTERN*

For Attorney General (Anglo Rep. versus Hispano Dem.)			For St. Treasurer (Both candidates Anglo)		No. Voting for Anglo Dem. but not for Hispano
Hispano Counties	Anglo Rep.	Hispano Dem.	Anglo Rep.	Anglo Dem.	
Rio Arriba	3475	5082	3563	4922	160
Taos	2303	3272	2325	3199	73
Valencia	2962	3584	3001	3575	9

Total voting in three Hispano
counties for Hispano Democrat,
but not for Anglo Democrat 242

*New Mexico Blue Book, 1952, published by New Mexico Secretary of State, Santa Fe, New Mexico.

ness among the Hispanos is found in Santa Fe County[4] with the following results in the same election for the same offices as above:

Anglo Rep.	Hispano Dem.	Anglo Rep.	Anglo Dem.
6,159	7,542	6,850	6,825

Hispano Democrats voting for Hispano
Democrats but not for Anglo Democrats

717

A still better guide to the evaluation of ethnic consciousness among New Mexico voters is found in the results of the primary election in 1950. With several candidates, both Anglo and Hispano, running under the same party label, the importance of political affiliation is eliminated. The four Hispano candidates running in the Democratic Primary in four "Anglo" counties for the office of secretary of state received about 25 per cent of the total votes cast, while the three Anglo candidates received about 75 per cent of the vote, as shown in Table VI. Where party "loyalty" was not a factor the Hispanos in the 1950 Democratic Primary were even more "racially" conscious than their fellow Anglo citizens, as can be seen in Table VII.

Anglo candidates received only about 10 per cent of the total votes cast in three "Hispano" counties for secretary of state in the Democratic Primary election; but where the reigning political machine

---

[4]New Mexico Secretary of State, New Mexico Blue Book (Santa Fe: Secretary of State Office, 1952) p. 19-20.

TABLE VI

VOTES CAST IN NEW MEXICO 1950 PRIMARY ELECTION SHOWING
AN ANGLO VOTING PATTERN IN A PRIMARY ELECTION*

Anglo Counties	Combined Vote of Four Hispano Candidates	Combined Vote of Three Anglo Candidates
Chavez	1,235	3,822
Curry	870	3,498
Eddy	1,530	4,350
Lea	428	4,425
Totals	4,063	16,095

*New Mexico Blue Book, 1952, published by New Mexico Secretary of State, Santa Fe, New Mexico.

TABLE VII

VOTES CAST IN NEW MEXICO 1950 PRIMARY ELECTION
SHOWING AN ANGLO VOTING BEHAVIOR PATTERN
IN A PRIMARY ELECTION*

Hispano Counties	Combined Vote of Four Hispano Candidates	Combined Vote of Three Anglo Candidates
Mora	947	57
Rio Arriba	3275	351
Taos	2150	218
San Miguel	3620	465
Totals	9992	1091

*New Mexico Blue Book, 1952, published by New Mexico Secretary of State, Santa Fe, New Mexico.

puts on the pressure, most Hispanos "stay in line." This is borne out
by the following figures on the race between John E. Miles, the machine
candidate for nomination for governor in the Democratic Primary and
Judge David Chavez, very popular among the Hispanos and a brother of the
late United States Senator, Dennis Chavez:

Hispano Counties	John E. Miles	David Chavez
Mora	485	590
San Miguel	2,106	2,296
Guadalupe	664	556
Taos	451	840
Rio Arriba	1,238	2,604
Totals	4,944	6,886

The large Anglo vote in New Mexico received by the late Congress-
man, Antonio Fernandez, is a notable exception to the general aversion
Anglos have to voting for Hispano candidates. But Fernandez had built
a solid reputation for protecting the economic interests of those classes
of the population in which Anglos predominate, such as cattle growers,
cotton farmers, oil men, and large real estate operators. He had won a
good proportion of the Anglo vote by voting against labor, rent controls,
and social security measures. In addition, he never attempted to protect
the rights of his own people and frequently disassociated himself from
them and their interests. The Anglo vote for Fernandez was, in large
measure, just a case of economic interests transcending other considerations.

The cultural conflict projects itself into the actual administration of government. Some departments in the state government, such as the Motor Vehicle and Land Office departments have been unofficially known as "Mexican" departments; others, such as the Highway and Tourist Departments are known as "Anglo" departments. Very few Hispanos, if any, are employed in Anglo departments and few Anglos in "Mexican" departments, although in recent years the "Mexican" departments are headed by Anglos, a distinct departure from tradition, but indicative of the fast waning political power of the Hispano Americans, a trend which just now shows signs of being reversed.

The Emerging Pattern in Other Southwestern States

Since 1947 a new picture is emerging. With World War II came physical mobility, resulting in the widening of horizons. Since that war, there has been a great deal of social mobility as well, on the part of the Hispanos, and greater efforts to educate members of this group.[5] Recent developments in Anglo-Hispano political relations and the increasing "ethnic consciousness" of the Hispano indicate new patterns of voting behavior by the Hispano in several southwestern states and a changing political role and political self-concept. In the presidential election

---

[5]In Denver between 1947 and 1959, the total number of Spanish name persons listed in the city directory increased by 48%, whereas the number of skilled workers increased by 70% (438 in 1947, 1380 in 1959); in 1948, only 94 out of 3,058 high school students were Hispanos, but in 1960, over 200 of 3,755 were Hispanos. In addition, the G. I. Bill, scholarships by the League of United Latin American Citizens in Colorado, New Mexico, Texas, and California, and the Latin American Educational Foundation in Denver have made it possible for a larger number of Hispanos to continue studies beyond the high school.

of 1960, for the first time in over one hundred years, the Hispanos
were organized as an effective national political block. PASSO (Political Association of Spanish Speaking Organizations) was organized by
Hispanos with the help and encouragement of the Kennedy forces as an
effective political arm of the Kennedy campaign organization. PASSO is
growing in importance and increasing its activities and areas of political action. Its leadership is young, energetic, well educated, union-
oriented, and left-wing.

The Democratic National Committee now has a Spanish Speaking
section,[6] and the drive by Hispanos for political recognition and representation has been launched on several broad fronts:

1. Demands for greater representation and participation
   in the party organizations and on governmental boards.
2. Organized registration drives to increase the number of
   Hispanos registered to vote.
3. Whenever necessary, placing "ethnic loyalty" above party
   loyalty.
4. Training in democratic procedures and political action
   techniques and tactics.

Hispano leaders and organizations are trying to make the Hispano both "ethnic" and "issue" conscious. Public forums, leadership
training institutes, discussion groups, and lectures are held often in
cities like Denver, Albuquerque, Santa Fe, San Antonio, Phoenix, and Los
Angeles, stressing the need for unity, participation in the political
and civic life of the communities, and appealing to ethnicentric fea-

---

[6]Carlos McCormack, a Mexican-American from Los Angeles and one
of the founders of PASSO heads the Spanish speaking unit.

tures of Hispanic culture.[7] One of the most interesting aspects of this training activity is the work being done with high school students who are drawn to various homes of leaders for long "bull sessions" on issues affecting them as Hispanos and the extensive history background offered these students by leaders who extoll the past glories of Hispanic greatness.

The following is an account of some of the most important recent developments in the Hispano's fast accelerating demands for political equality and political recognition and his growing importance as a political force in several American states. The most dramatic and most recent manifestation of the increasing "ethnic" consciousness of the Hispano occurred on April 13, 1963 at Crystal City, Texas. In this town of some 10,000 inhabitants, the Hispanos, although constituting a clear majority of the town's citizens, had never had an important voice in the town's government. Following a vigorous campaign to have the Hispanos pay their poll tax and register to vote, the Hispanos outnumbered the Anglo registered voters by almost two to one. On election day, the Hispanos elected everyone of their candidates for the town council. For a complete account of the background and the election that followed, see the articles which appeared in two national magazines and one national newspaper.[8]

---

[7] In Denver, several organizations, including the Latin American Federation Luncheon Club, hold monthly meetings and sponsor weekly discussion groups.

[8] See Appendix A for reproduction of these articles.

The 1962 Gubernatorial Election in Colorado

In Colorado, in the 1962 gubernatorial election, the Hispano
appears to have manifested a greater degree of ethnicity than he is
known to have shown in any previous election since statehood (1876).
Although analysis of voting statistics for this election indicates that
there was a degree of defection from the Democratic Party on the part of
the general population, the defection on the part of Hispanos seems to
have been so much greater in certain precincts and clustering of precincts
with a significant number of Hispano voters that it was possible to hypo-
thesize that certain factors, unique to the emerging Hispano-dominate
political relations, were in operation during this election.

For the first time in Colorado history, the Hispanos had their
own state-wide newspaper, "El Tiempo," published weekly in Denver.[9] For
the first time as far as it is known, the question of the rights of Hispanos became a major political issue, forced upon the attention of both
parties and the public in general. For the first time, one of the major
political parties capitalized on a state-wide basis on the "ethnic consciousness" of the Hispano voters of Colorado. One of the questions we
attempt to answer in this study is whether the "ethnic" issue was an effective one. See Appendix B for an abstract of votes cast in the gubernatorial race.

---

[9]"El Tiempo" is a militant weekly newspaper. Its editor, Dr. Daniel
T. Valdes, has always been a liberal Democrat and the paper consistently
has followed a liberal point of view. During the 1962 elections, 20,000
Hispano families were receiving the paper, distributed mostly by Republican
precinct workers.

The most significant results were found in the traditional home
of the Hispano, southern Colorado. Pueblo, site of the large steel mills
of the Colorado Fuel and Iron Corporation, a labor and Democratic strong-
hold, went Democratic except in the governor's race where McNichols lost
to the Republican nominee, Governor John Love. John Carroll, running for
the United States Senate, won over his Republican opponent by nearly
4,000 votes; Democrats elected all four state representatives by substantial majorities and a state senator by a 10,000 plurality. But Love
defeated McNichols by 6,256 votes. In very heavy Democratic "Anglo" precincts McNichols received 58 per cent of the vote, while in very heavy
Democratic "Hispano" precincts he received only 46 per cent of the vote.
Table VIII shows precinct by precinct votes in all the most heavily Democratic precincts in Pueblo County in the gubernatorial race, comparing
"Hispano" and "Anglo" precincts. See, also, Appendix C.

In Las Animas County, almost 100 per cent Democratic and predominantly Hispano (see Table IX for number of Spanish surname whites in
selected areas of Colorado), McNichols won by only 1,109 votes on a total
vote of 8,679, whereas just six years ago he won the county by more than
3,000 votes. In Denver where the greatest concentration of Hispanos in
the state is found, the findings, at least on the surface, are conflicting.
On the basis of actual voting statistics by election precincts and districts, there appears to have been only a little more than a four per
cent defection on the part of Hispanos from the Democratic Party toward
a vote for the Republican candidate for governor. This four per cent

TABLE VIII

VOTES CAST IN PUEBLO COUNTY, COLORADO
1962 GUBERNATORIAL ELECTION

U. S. Census Tracts	Hispano Precincts*	Vote For Love	McNichols
8	18	206	162
	19	210	253
	30	337	158
	31	255	166
10	25	219	178
	27	236	210
	29	315	141
12	28	232	168
	33	360	272
	34	201	300
20	38	168	133
	50	163	245
	48	207	251
21	72	199	314
		3,308	2,951

U. S. Census Tracts	Anglo Precincts**	Vote For Love	McNichols
19, 24	38	168	333
	71	255	301
	73	150	307
	74	256	222
3	11	149	170
19	12	247	293
	51	104	254
	52	123	276
		1,452	2,056

Percentage of votes to McNichols
  Hispano precincts   46.9
  Anglo precincts   58.6

*20 to 65 per cent Hispano, over 65 per cent Democratic.

**Less than 10 per cent Hispano, over 65 per cent Democratic.

TABLE IX

NUMBER OF PERSONS OF SPANISH SURNAMES
IN SELECTED COLORADO AREAS*

Total population and white population of Spanish surname for Standard
Metropolitan Statistical Areas in Colorado:

SMSA	Population Total	Spanish Surname
Denver	929,383	60,294
Colorado Springs	143,742	6,135
Pueblo	118,707	25,437

Urban places of 10,000 or more with 2,500 or more white persons of Spanish surname:

Urban Place	Population Total	Spanish Surname
Colorado Springs	70,194	3,471
Denver	493,887	43,147
Pueblo	91,181	16,036
Trinidad	10,691	3,688

Colorado counties with 2,500 or more white persons of Spanish surname:

County	Spanish Surname	County	Spanish Surname
Adams	8,542	Jefferson	2,515
Arapahoe	2,987	Las Animas	7,443
Boulder	3,103	Mesa	2,612
Conejos	4,476	Otero	5,328
Costilla	3,065	Pueblo	25,437
Denver	43,147	Rio Grande	3,477
El Paso	6,135	Weld	8,831
Huerfano	3,608		

*Source: 1960 United States Census.

defection in election districts having 25 to 50 per cent Hispano population compares with less than one and one half per cent defection in
comparable (in social, economic status) election districts with .0 per
cent to 10 per cent Hispano population. Table X shows votes in the
Colorado races for governor and U. S. Senator.. Also, see Appendix D.
Thus the defection to Love, the Republican candidate, in areas with
large numbers of Hispano voters is several times greater than in areas
with little or practically no Hispano voters. But both percentages are
much too small to be really significant. It is very important to keep
in mind, however, that since Hispanos constitute only 25 to 50 per cent
of the population in so-called Hispano districts, the four per cent defection may have been much larger but did not show in the total votes
cast for governor in each district. As a matter of fact, this suppo-
sition is supported by the results of the interviews of Hispano voters
during the panel survey conducted for this thesis. The panel survey shows
that 33 per cent of Hispanos interviewed and living in these districts,
said they had voted for Love. Only 5 per cent of those who said they
voted for Love said they had done so because he was a Republican.

Therefore, 28.8 per cent defected from the Democratic party to
vote for Love. Table XI shows how the Hispano respondents answered the
following question: "For whom did you vote in the last election?"
McNichols ___, Love ___, Why? ___

It is significant that of the respondents (98 per cent Democrats)
who stated they had voted for Love, 47.4 per cent said they did so be-

TABLE X

VOTES CAST IN DENVER, COLORADO 1962 GUBERNATORIAL ELECTION*
SHOWING DEGREE OF HISPANO DEFECTION FROM
DEMOCRATIC PARTY IN DENVER

"Hispano" Electoral Districts**					"Anglo" Electoral Districts***				
Dist.	Love	McNichols	Dominick	Carroll	Dist.	Love	McNichols	Dominick	Carroll
2	1448	3729	1241	3904	1	1904	2518	1872	2591
3	841	2392	752	2593	4	2096	2321	1999	2406
5	1711	2387	1662	2436	6	2319	2593	2218	2687
7	1503	2927	1339	3112	4	2182	2493	2047	2610
10	955	2412	764	2564	16	1245	2805	1128	2913
11	1829	2360	1640	2515	24	1779	1805	1771	1794
12	1735	2387	1463	2657					
13	2587	3045	2319	3294					
T	12,609	21,641	10,990	23,075	T	12,525	14,535	12,035	15,001

Total votes cast in
8 "Hispano" Districts   34,250

Votes cast, Carroll over McNichols   1,434

Total votes cast in
6 "Anglo" Districts   27,060

Votes cast, Carroll over McNichols   466

*Official election results reported by Colorado Secretary of State.

**25 to 50 per cent of registered voters have Spanish surnames.

***0 to 10 per cent of registered voters have Spanish surnames.

TABLE XI

VOTES CAST BY HISPANOS FOR LOVE AND McNICHOLS
IN 1962 GUBERNATORIAL ELECTION*

McNichols 144   Love 84

   Percentage . . . . 58.2%   Percentage 33.8%

   Did not vote 12   Percentage 8.0%

   Refused to answer 8

Reasons given by respondents for voting for candidates:

	Love	McNichols
Party	N4, 4.8%	N92, 63.3%
"Best man"	N28, 33.3%	N38, 26.4%
"Best for our people"	N40, 47.6%	N10, 6.9%
"Time for a change"	N8, 9.5%	
"Other"	N4, 4.8%	N4, 3.4%
	84 100%	144 100%

*Based on respondents' information.

cause Love was "best for our people." Only 6.9 per cent who said they voted for McNichols said they voted for him because he was "best for our people." As a matter of fact, 63.8 per cent said they voted for McNichols becuase he was a Democrat, but only 5 per cent said they voted for Love because he was a Republican.[10]

---

[10]From first interview schedule. See Appendix E.

CHAPTER VI

THE POPULATION AND THE
LOCALE OF THE RESEARCH PROJECT

Distribution of Hispanos in the Area of the Project

A brief outline of the locale, the population and background
events will help to understand better the study and the findings and
interpretations resulting from the research project.[1] Denver is a
cosmopolitan city in that almost every racial, ethnic, and nationality
group can be found within its geographical limits. According to the
1960 census, the City and County of Denver has a population of nearly
one-half million. Of these, the majority are so-called Anglo-Saxon
Protestants, but other ethnic, racial, and religious groups form a
substantial proportion, estimated at 30 per cent of the city's population.[2] This is divided approximately into the following major racial,
ethnic, and religious groups:

	City Proper	Metropolitan Area
Jews	21,000	32,000
Whites with Spanish Surnames	43,147	60,000
Italian-Americans	40,000	45,000
Negroes	32,000	32,000
	136,147	169,000

----

[1] The specific sample and research area are shown on Table XIV.

[2] Based on 1960 population census; estimates based on school populations, church census figures, and figures kept by foreign consulates
in Denver.

It is estimated that five out of every ten persons living in Denver were born elsewhere, the majority outside of the State of Colorado.[3]

Denver, the locale of the study, is an important center of Hispano population.[4] In Metropolitan Denver, the Hispano population was, according to the 1960 census, nearly 60,000, making up 7 per cent of the population of the four county metropolitan area.[5] Seventy-five per cent of these White persons having Spanish surnames live in the central city (within the City and County of Denver), making up 15 per cent of the population within the City and County limits. About 65 per cent of the Hispanos are found in four areas of the city. See Figure 2 for distribution in Denver Metropolitan area of members of this culture group.

The City and County of Denver is divided politically into 37 districts. What concentrations there are of Hispanos are found in the following districts:

Districts 2, 3, 5, and 15
(Northwest Denver — 8,502 Hispanos)

Districts 7, 9, 10, and 11
(West and Southwest Denver — 10,728 Hispanos)

------

[3]Of the 6,075 prominent persons listed in the 1958 edition of Who's Who in Colorado, only 1,675 gave their birthplace as Colorado.

[4]The ten cities in the Southwest with the largest population of Spanish surname and the number of such persons in 1960, were Los Angeles, 260,389; San Antonio, 243,627; El Paso, 125,745; East Los Angeles, 70,802; Houston, 63,372; Corpus Christi, 59,859; San Francisco, 51,602; Laredo, 49,819; Albuquerque, 43,790; and Denver, 43,147.

[5]"Population Report," Denver Planning Office, 1962, City and County of Denver.

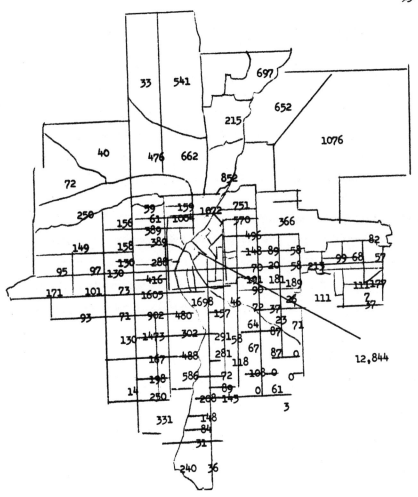

FIGURE 2

DISTRIBUTION AND CONCENTRATION OF PERSONS
WITH SPANISH SURNAME, DENVER
METROPOLITAN AREA, 1960

Districts 3 and 20
(Downtown-west side — 6,591 Hispanos)

Districts 3 and 18
(Downtown-east side — 10,564 Hispanos)

In addition about 19,000 Hispanos are scattered throughout the
City and County of Denver. See Figure 2. Nearly 75 per cent of the
Hispanos in the concentrated areas are registered Democrats, a little
less than 15 per cent unaffiliated, and 10 per cent Republicans.[6]

Socio-economic background of Denver Hispanos. The first White settlers
in Colorado were Spanish. The oldest White settlement in what is now
Colorado is the Spanish village of San Luis, located in the San Luis
Valley of Southern Colorado. In 1845 these people became American citizens, a status ratified by the terms of the Treaty of Guadalupe Hidalgo.
The great majority of the Spanish-speaking people of Denver are descendents of these early Americans. These people developed the first agriculture in Colorado, initiated livestock raising and taught the Anglos
how to mine for gold and other metals. They founded the first churches
and the first schools in the state and were found among the drafters and
signers of the Colorado Constitution and were active in territorial
politics.[7]

---

[6]Spot check of 1962 registration lists.

[7]Katherine Kenehan, Colorado - The Land and the People (Denver
Public Schools, 1957) p. 10.

With the increasing influx of Anglo farmers and merchants into the southern part of Colorado and the rapid development of the northern section of the state due to mining and railroad developments, the Hispano (the term Mexican is still used by the uninformed and the biased Anglo in referring to these Americans) rapidly lost ground, politically, culturally, and economically. Division of family landholdings among numerous succeeding sons, without new development of agricultural lands, soon reduced the once independent and proud Spanish farmer and stock grower to marginal farming. Long before the great depression of the 1930's many of these people began to travel to the northern counties as seasonal migratory workers in the fruit growing and beet-raising areas of the Western Slope and the Greeley-Longmont areas of the state.

The first permanent Spanish speaking settlers in Denver were these migratory workers who never went back to their southern Colorado homes but remained in Denver to be nearer to the areas where they could find, at least, part-time employment. Unlike the bulk of the peoples of other racial, ethnic, and religious classifications who came as railroad workers, factory workers, farmers, miners, skilled workers and merchants, the foundation of the Spanish speaking population of Denver was the unskilled, the uneducated rural small farmer, demoralized and poverty stricken, accepting most any conditions to supplement (and in many cases to acquire total subsistence) his meager income from his overworked and tiny plots of land in southern Colorado. Then came the great depression of the 1930's and there was a great exodus of these people from New

Mexico, the San Luis Valley, and the Walsenburg and Trinidad areas of
Colorado.[8] Mortgages were foreclosed on their farms, their houses were
sold for delinquent taxes, part-time labor in the small towns disappeared.
In addition, the economically-poor and politically-weak southern counties
were not able to give the assistance and work relief offered by the City
and County of Denver. It is estimated that there were less than 5,000
Hispanos living in Denver in 1930 and that more than 12,000 came to Denver
between 1930 and 1940. The greatest, and latest migration to Denver
occurred during, and following, World War II. During this period the Hispano population of Denver almost tripled in size.[9] War and miscellaneous
factories and plants, and the mushrooming service and food processing industries which were necessary to serve the tremendous wartime growth all
offered unprecedented opportunities for those willing to accept relatively
low wages and those who were unskilled to be offered better jobs.

Since World War II, Hispanos have continued to come to Denver in
unusually large numbers, only now tapering off because the small towns
and villages and farms of southern Colorado have been practically de-
populated of these people. The only ones remaining are the older people,
most of them receiving pensions; relatively well-off small farmers, those
who have gotten comparatively well-paying, white collar jobs in the

---

[8]Daniel T. Valdes, Spanish People of the Southwest; illustrated
monograph, Colorado State Department of Education, 1940, p. 9.

[9]1950 United States Census.

small towns and those working for city and county governments. Practically
the only ones now leaving these areas for Denver are the young people,
looking for better opportunities in the larger cities.

The Mexican-Americans living in Denver are almost evenly divided
between those who are second and third generation descendents of Mexicans
who came to the United States following the long and turbulent Mexican Revolution of 1911, and the years following and those who are recent immigrants
to the United States. The early comers to Denver were mostly those who
had originally come to the United States as agricultural laborers and railroad track workers, many gravitating to Denver and settling here. But
many of these, also, returned to their native country during the depression
of the 1930's when Anglo workers, desperate for work, began to accept the
back-breaking agricultural field and railroad track work, throwing the
Mexicans upon the mercy of local relief agencies who refused to help them.
The United States and Mexican governments cooperatively provided transporta-
tion back to their homes in Mexico. Of those who remained in the United
States, many have never become American citizens. It is estimated that
over half of the Mexicans in Denver (all those of comparatively recent
Mexican origin) have never gotten their citizenship papers, and nearly all
Americans of Mexican origin who have become American citizens have become
so by birth.[10]

---

[10]Estimate made by Mexican Consul in Denver.

Official police records kept by the City and County of Denver do not differentiate between the "Spanish-American" and the "Mexican" in recording and reporting persons arrested. All are listed under "Spanish" and differentiated from "Whites."[11]

During the year, 1960, 26,323 persons were arrested in Denver for 24 or more offenses ranging from "suspicion" to "murder" but excluding traffic violations. Although "Spanish-Americans" and "Mexicans" constitute less than 15 per cent of the population, over 28 per cent of those arrested are listed as "Spanish" on official police records. The percentage of "Spanish" is particularly high in the number of persons arrested for burglary (over 50 per cent of the total number arrested); larceny and theft (48 per cent); auto theft (61 per cent); and drunkenness (29 per cent).

A smaller percentage of "Spanish" than the overall average (28 per cent) for this group are arrested for murder and manslaughter. Hispanos commit only 20 per cent of the murders and manslaughter in the city. For the rest of the offenses, the "Spanish" do not commit more than their share and sometimes less: embezzlement, 11 per cent; prostitution and commercial vice, 11 per cent; sex offenses, 16 per cent; and gambling, 6 per cent. See Table XII for a breakdown of offenses by ethnic and racial group.

_____

[11]Records Bureau, Denver Police Department Annual Report, 1960.

TABLE XII

ARRESTS IN CITY AND COUNTY OF DENVER, 1960
BY ETHNIC AND RACIAL GROUPS*

Offense	White	Negro	Indian	Yellow	Spanish	Total
Murder & Non-Negligent						
Manslaughter	11	9			5	25
Manslaughter by Negligence	8	1			2	11
Forcible Rape	6	6			11	23
Robbery	57	66	2		51	176
Aggravated Assault	30	42	1		32	105
Burglary	253	105	6	1	345	710
Larceny-Theft	608	244	8	3	443	1,306
Auto Theft	184	29		2	340	555
Other Assaults	96	47			68	211
Forgery	38	6			21	65
Embezzlement	241	41	3	1	39	325
Stolen Property	4	7			6	17
Carrying Weapons	66	108	2		66	242
Prostitution & Comm. Vice	94	90	2		24	210
Sex Offenses	233	126	6	1	71	437
Offenses Against Family						
& Children	13	3			10	26
Narcotic Laws	26	40	1		59	126
Liquor Laws	69	12			36	117
Drunkenness	7,585	996	578	17	3,321	12,497
Disorderly Conduct	278	109	8	1	145	541
Vagrancy	166	68	3	2	62	301
Gambling	36	61			7	104
Driving While Intoxicated	477	83	3		136	699
Suspicion	795	602	15	5	760	2,177
All Others except Traffic	3,008	758	41	8	1,502	5,317
TOTAL	14,382	3,659	679	41	7,562	26,323

*From official Denver Police Department records.

The average income of the Hispanos living in Denver is estimated to be 75 per cent of the average of the total population. There are many from this group working in unionized factories and plants and for the city, state, and federal governments (earning close to that of the general population), but the overall average or percentage for the group as a whole is dramatically lowered by the comparatively large number still earning 55 cents to 75 cents an hour (in agriculture, restaurants, hotels, and paper processing companies). There is also a comparatively large number of these people whose only income is from old-age assistance or aid to dependent children. The average yearly income for the Hispano in Denver is estimated at $3,200 compared to an average of $4,500 for the total population.[11]

To a greater extent than any other minority, this group presents the greatest "problem" in education. There is alarming absenteeism from schools, late registrations, and early withdrawals. There are proportionately fewer high school graduates from this group than from any other groups studied. In addition to low economic status, discriminatory practices against them, poor housing, and poor health, many children from this group, also must struggle against language barriers created in homes where only (or most often) Spanish is spoken.

"Drop-outs" from schools are greatest in this group; greater even than among Negroes. School authorities tend to attribute this to lack

----

[11]1960 United States Census. See Denver Population Report (Denver: Denver Planning Office, 1961).

of education of parents and their relatively recent arrival from educa-
tion-poor rural areas.[12]   The number of "Spanish" students in colleges
and universities is distressingly low.

Denver now has 3,212 family living units in 11 low-cost housing
projects located within its city limits. Of these, the Lincoln Park
Project, located near the business district on West Colfax, the J. Q.
Newton Project, and the Sun Valley Homes, both situated in northwest
Denver, have more than a third of these units. Spanish-name families
occupy 1,371 of the total units in the 11 projects, representing nearly
43 per cent of all low-cost housing units in the city.[13]   Table XIII
shows the distribution of ethnic groups in Denver public housing units.

---

[12]School Statistics, A Report Prepared by The School Board, City
and County of Denver (Denver: Board of Education, 1962).

[13]Denver Housing Authority 1962 report.

TABLE XIII

DISTRIBUTION BY ETHNIC AND RACIAL GROUPS OF RESIDENTS OF PUBLIC HOUSING UNITS, CITY AND COUNTY OF DENVER, 1961

	Las Casitas (184)		Lincoln Pk. (422)		Platte Vly-Curtis Pk. (293)		Arapahoe Ct-Curtis Pk. (310)		Columbine (200)		West Rdge. (200)		J. Q. Newton (400)	
	No.	%	No.	%	No.	%	No.	%	No.	%	No.	%	No.	%
Anglo	37	20.6	161	38.7	5	1.7	12	3.9	157	78.9	90	45.5	179	45.0
Hispano	133	73.9	182	43.8	48	16.4	125	40.6	35	17.6	75	37.9	183	46.0
Negro	5	2.8	67	16.1	238	81.5	171	55.5	5	2.5	23	11.6	32	8.0
Indian, Oriental	5	2.8	6	1.4	1	.3	0	0.0	2	1.0	10	5.0	4	1.0
TOTAL	180	100.0	416	100.0	292	100.0	308	100.0	199	100.0	198	100.0	398	100.0
Earned	122	67.8	310	74.5	213	74.9	195	63.3	160	80.4	134	67.6	289	72.6
Unearned (Welfare)	49	27.2	101	24.3	67	22.9	102	33.1	25	12.6	61	30.8	97	24.4
Combination	9	5.0	5	1.2	12	4.1	11	3.6	14	7.0	3	1.5	12	3.0
TOTAL	180	100.0	292	100.0	308	100.0	199	100.0	198	100.0	198	100.0	398	100.0

Source: Denver Housing Authority, 1960 Report

TABLE XIII (Continued)

	Sun Valley (420)		So. Lincoln (270)		Westwood (257)		B. Stapleton (290)		Total DHA Program (3246)	
	No.	%	No.	%	No.	%	No.	%	No.	%
Anglo	133	31.9	55	20.4	135	52.5	39	14.1	1003	31.2
Hispano	208	49.9	163	60.4	98	38.1	121	43.7	1371	42.7
Negro	61	14.6	48	17.8	16	6.2	111	40.1	777	24.2
Indian, Oriental	15	3.6	4	1.5	8	3.1	6	2.2	61	1.9
TOTAL	417	100.0	270	100.0	257	100.0	277	100.0	3212	100.0
Earned	312	74.8	184	68.1	181	70.4	181	65.3	2281	71.0
Unearned (Welfare)	93	22.3	81	30.0	70	27.2	81	29.2	827	25.8
Combination	12	2.9	5	1.9	6	2.3	15	5.4	104	3.2
TOTAL	417	100.0	270	100.0	257	100.0	277	100.0	3212	100.0

THE RESEARCH PROJECT

The research is an attempt to secure basic data in order to proceed from knowledge about discrete phenomena at the microscopic level (individual voting) to some macroscopic picture (role of a sub or contra-culture in the total political system). The research is aimed at analytic knowledge derived from interview studies among individual Hispano voters. The major problem was to work up to possible theories at the system level so as to develop a macroscopic picture of the cultural sub-system of the Hispano cultural group as it functions within the larger or total social system, more specifically, in the total political system. The research also attempts to determine when and how voters in this cultural group make up their minds, resulting in overt behavior at the polls. It was the aim of the research to construct theories that would combine and explain discrete findings from which valid hypotheses could be deduced. These propositions were tested upon data secured from interviews, and election statistics, and analyzed within historical perspectives and backgrounds.

The Survey and the Research Hypotheses

The research itself, is both a descriptive and explanatory survey. It measured precisely many secondary dependent variables but primarily the dependent variable, voting behavior, in a representative sample of Spanish-name Americans in the City and County of Denver who were registered to vote in the 1962 Denver municipal election.[1] It

seeks to establish the relationship between the dependent variable and

the hypothesized causes or independent variables, ethnicity and ex -

posure to selected mass media communication.

The general objectives of the research are:

1. To understand better the present role and voting behavior of Hispanos in the United States political
system.
2. To provide accurate information for future and expanded
research in the field of political sociology.
3. To obtain a clearer understanding of what decreases
and increases citizenship efficiency and democratic
voting behavior in an important ethnic population.

The following are the research hypotheses based on previous

experience of the writer, on previous cursory knowledge, and extensive

contacts with the group which is the focus of the study:

Research Hypothesis #1 (H_1)

Americans with Spanish surnames with higher degrees of ethnicity

are more likely to take or change positions during an election campaign

toward an ethnically approved candidate than toward an ethnically unac-

ceptable candidate.

Research Hypothesis #2 (H_2)

Americans with Spanish surnames with high ethnicity and with

---

[1] Data were collected during three interviews that could be used to
test additional hypotheses not included in this report.

greater exposure to "ethnic oriented" propaganda are more likely to
take or change positions toward ethnically acceptable candidates.

Research Hypothesis #3 (H_3)

The number of respondents with low ethnicity who will change
or take positions favorable to ethnically acceptable candidates will be
greater than the number who will change or take a position toward an
ethnically unfavorable candidate.

Research Hypothesis #4 (H_4)

The number of respondents with low ethnicity but high exposure
to selected mass media communication who change or take positions favorable to ethnically acceptable candidates will be greater than the
number who change or take a position favorable toward ethnically unac-
ceptable candidates.

Research Hypothesis #5 (H_5)

During the election campaign more ethnically oriented respondents
will change to greater interest in the election than the Anglo oriented
respondents.

Research Hypothesis #6 (H_6)

During the election campaign more ethnically oriented respondents
will change toward greater intention to vote than Anglo oriented respondents.

Research Hypothesis #7 (H_7)

During the election campaign more ethnically oriented respondents with high exposure to selected mass media communication will change toward greater interest in the election than Anglo oriented respondents with high exposure to selected mass media communication.

Research Hypothesis #8 (H$_8$)

During the election campaign more ethnically oriented respondents with high exposure to selected mass media communication will change toward greater intention to vote than Anglo oriented respondents with high exposure to selected mass media communication.

The population and the sample. About 37,000 Americans with Spanish names live in the 25 United States Census tracts which establish the boundaries of the setting of the survey. There are 54 United States Census tracts in the City and County of Denver. Twenty-one tracts, all located in the City and County of Denver, are included in the study. This area roughly includes eight of the thirty-seven election districts in the City and County of Denver. Figure 3 shows the eight election districts with heavy concentration of Spanish name registered voters.

The frame for the probability sample was the latest official voter registration lists prepared by the Election Commission of the City and County of Denver. The lists were up-to-date as of March, 1963, just two months before the survey was undertaken. From a random start by the interval method the sample was drawn from the official registration lists containing names of registered voters in forty precincts in these eight election districts which were chosen because of the relatively heavy con-

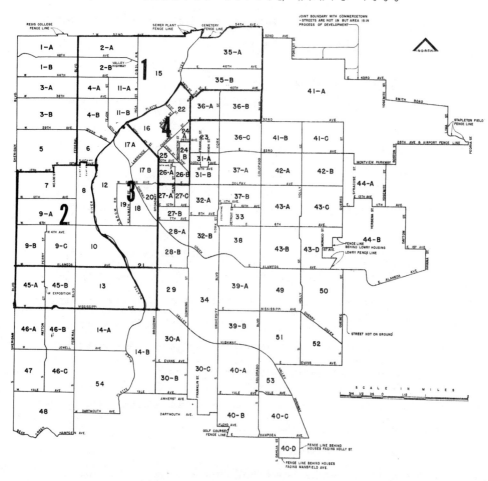

1960 CENSUS TRACTS, DENVER

DENVER PLANNING OFFICE, APRIL 1960

FIGURE 3

AREAS OF CONCENTRATION OF HISPANOS IN CITY OF DENVER

NOTE: Area 1 - 8,502 Hispanos; Area 2 - 10,728 Hispanos; Area 3 - 6,591 Hispanos; Area 4 - 10,564 Hispanos. Total - 36,385.

centration of Americans with Spanish surnames in the precincts. The registration lists supplied the name, address, and party affiliation or non-affiliation of all registered voters in these precincts. These forty precincts had a total of 22,568 registered voters of whom 6,756 were Americans with Spanish surnames. Every twentieth Spanish surname on these lists was selected for the sample. The selection of the names was done by the writer, who is thoroughly familiar with Spanish names because of his background and his familiarity with Spanish history, literature, and the historical origins of the names. The result was a sample population of registered voters with Spanish surnames. Table XIV lists the precincts included in the survey, the total number of registered voters, and the number of registered voters with Spanish surnames in each precinct.

Since only registered voters can translate "ethnic consciousness" into effective political behavior by voting, the exclusions involved all non-citizens,[2] all non-registered potential voters and female and male adults under twenty-one years of age.

Mortality or loss of respondents due to refusals, moving away, et cetera, in the first wave of interviewing reduced the sample to 285 registered voters. This number was further reduced to 245 in the second wave of interviews. The third post-election wave of interviews reduced the figure still more for the final total of respondents of 208 registered

---

[2] According to the 1960 U. S. Census, there were 977 "foreignborn" persons with Spanish surnames in the 21 census tracts in the survey. See Appendix F.

TABLE XIV

110

EXACT LISTING OF PRECINCTS IN THE PANEL SURVEY*

Precinct	Total Reg. Voters	Total Reg. Hispanos	In Sample
203	527	240	12
204	322	140	7
205	553	441	21
206	357	318	17
207	536	300	15
208	658	100	5
209	583	365	17
212	581	160	8
213	743	163	8
214	691	105	5
301	289	160	8
302	776	335	16
303	731	220	11
305	616	395	20
306	685	400	21
307	358	101	5
308	430	100	5
309	389	45	2
310	430	200	10
312	505	223	12
703	522	204	10
710	704	143	7
711	955	160	8
712	572	125	6
901	582	120	6
903	614	65	3
905	615	131	6
1006	599	180	9
1007	504	143	7
1010	555	200	10
1011	484	141	13
1102	466	85	4
1108	718	40	2
1112	715	47	2
1107	633	65	3
1206	667	79	4
1209	647	131	6
1211	590	65	3
1501	337	59	3
1502	429	62	3
40 Precincts	22,568	6,756	340 Respondents

*Also see Appendix G.

voters. All data secured during the three interviews and referred to in
the findings and conclusions of this report refer to the final residue of
208 respondents or households since only one member of the household or
family was sampled and interviewed and only the same respondent was re-
interviewed. These 208 respondents constituted the panel. Of the initial
total of 340 in the sample, 55 were never interviewed because of repeated
failure to find the persons at home, refusal to answer all or a substantial
portion of the questionnaire, sickness, or wrong or nonexistent persons
listed in the registration lists. This represented an initial mortality
of 16.1 per cent. The final mortality rate was 39.8 per cent.

The Hispano group, as well as the Anglo group, in the research area,
was expected to be predominantly oriented towards the Democratic Party and
this was borne out by the large proportion of persons registered as Democrats. In the electoral districts within the research area, 60.4 per cent
of the registered voters were registered as Democrats, 11.1 per cent as
Republicans, and 26.5 per cent as unaffiliated voters. Table XV shows
the total number of voters registered as Democrats, Republicans, and unaffiliated voters and the percentage of Spanish name voters in each of the
electoral districts in the research area..

The panel technique.

This technique involved interviewing the same group of people on
three different occasions. The panel technique consisted of making more
than one contact with the groups being surveyed. Compared to other methods
for securing data, the panel technique is of recent origin. It has been

TABLE XV

PARTY REGISTRATION FIGURES IN DISTRICTS
IN THE SURVEY*

Electoral Districts	Percentage of Hispanos	Registration		
		Republicans	Democrats	Unaffiliated
2	24.1%	801	5,070	2,229
3	20.2%	471	4,529	938
7	29.7%	883	4,417	2,200
9	10.0%	1,120	3,238	2,389
10	16.2%	577	4,014	1,273
11	10.2%	1,311	3,630	2,169
12	17.5%	1,052	3,799	2,320
15	34.2%	528	4,840	1,581
18	14.9%	520	4,005	1,127
Average	19.64% Total	7,263	37,542	16,226
		Grand Total	61,031	

*Source: Official Registration Lists, Election Commission, City
and County of Denver.

used in consumer surveys and principally in surveys on voting behavior.
Its major value lies in being able to obtain data indicating changes in
opinions, attitudes and values over a period of time and under observed
conditions. Mildred Parten lists the advantages and disadvantages of this
technique and concludes that, "The problems raised by the panel procedure
are often sufficient to offset the advantages".[3] However, Pauline V.
Young points out that it has the more or less unique advantage of studying
and tracing the specific developments of a social process, that is,
"...the progressive actions, factors, or attitudes which determine a given
behavior pattern or social situation."[4]

Although the first interview had already provided data for cor-
relating ethnicity and voting behavior in past elections, the panel technique was necessary to study changes in attitudes during a stated and definite period of time and under more or less controlled stimuli. This period of time was provided and measured by the length of the campaign during
the mayoralty election held in Denver on May 18, 1963. The cumulative
data from the three interviews would also provide further information on
the relationship between "ethnicity" among Hispanos and their voting behavior under conditions designed to stimulate "ethnicity." People in the
sample were interviewed before and after a mass communication campaign
calling attention to certain ideas. These ideas were presented in two

---

[3]Mildred Parten, Surveys, Polls, and Samples: Practical Procedures
(New York: Harper and Brothers, 1950), p. 99.

[4]Pauline V. Young, Scientific Social Surveys and Research
(Englewood Cliffs, New Jersey, 1956), pp. 212-213.

major forms: (1) a television speech calling attention to the present
mayor's (and one of the candidates) failure to eliminate discrimination
against Hispanos and his failure to stop police brutality aimed primarily
at persons from minority groups; (2) two issues of El Tiempo appealing to
the Hispanos' pride and the need to "throw out of office" those responsible
for their plight. (See Appendix H for the written text of the television
speech which was heard by an estimated 40,000 Hispanos in Denver and of
the articles in El Tiempo believed to have been read by some 30,000 Hispanos).

The first interviews for the pre-test were conducted the weekend
of April 5-6. Both telephone and house calls were used. The first interviews after the pre-test were completed on April 11-13 and April 18, 19,
and 20. In between these two dates (on April 13) the survey and the purpose
of the interviews was explained to a television audience estimated at
40,000 Hispanos. A front page article was carried in the weekly Hispano
newspaper, El Tiempo, also explaining the survey.[5] The second wave of
interviews was conducted on May 1, 2, 3, 4, and 5 and the post-election
interviews were conducted on May 29, 30, and 31. The marked calendar on
Figure 4 designates the dates relative to important phases of the research
project. The calendar also shows the number of intervals between waves
and the stimuli producing events.

_____

[5]See Appendix I.

APRIL, 1963

Sun.	Mon.	Tues.	Wed.	Thurs.	Fri.	Sat.	
	1	2	3	4	⑤	⑥	Pre-test
7	8	⑨	⑩	⑪	⑫	⑬	First regular interviews
14	15	16	17	⑱	19	20	Election issue of "El Tiempo"
21	22	23	24	25	26	27	
㉘	29	30					Special TV Election Program

MAY, 1963

Sun.	Mon.	Tue.	Wed.	Thurs.	Fri.	Sat.	
			①	②	③	④	Second wave of interviews
⑤	6	7	8	9	10	11	
12	13	14	15	⑯	17	18	Election issue "El Tiempo"
19	20	㉑	22	23	24	25	Mayoralty election
26	27	28	㉙	㉚	㉛		Post-election interviews

FIGURE 4

DATES OF DIFFERENT PHASES OF THE PANEL SURVEY

Nature and Source of Data

The first questionnaire in the panel survey supplied the following basic information for each respondent for eventual comparison
with ethnicity and voting behavior: age, sex, education, associations,
church membership and attendance, occupation, income, and union affiliation. In addition, the first questionnaire provided information
relative to both subjective and objective criteria for gauging ethnic
and political orientation. Further, the first interview provided
information on voting intentions and factual knowledge of the respondents relative to the Denver mayoralty election.

Official City and County of Denver registration lists provided
the names, addresses, and political affiliations of the prospective
respondents. The United States Census data provided figures which
showed the extent of Spanish-named populations in the areas selected.
Official voting statistics provided voting data where needed.

The second pre-election interview provided data on changes in
factual knowledge regarding the mayoralty election and changes in voting intentions. This interview also showed exposure to various types
of mass media communication dealing with the election and the issues
and personalities involved.

The last or post-election interview also provided data showing
change or lack of change in voting intention and knowledge of the election and the candidates. But most important, this reinterview produced
information indicating if and how the respondent finally voted and why.

Conceptual Variables

The first step in the planning of the survey must consist in laying out as specifically and clearly as possible the conceptual system that will guide the survey. This is necessary to avoid collecting just a set of interesting but unrelated facts. An adequate set of concepts must be developed before the collection of interviews in order to have a clearly formulated idea of what kind of facts are needed, to be able to recognize the facts and know why the facts are needed.

Ethnicity. This is an awareness of being a part of an externally classified category of persons. To survive, a society must inculcate in each of its members a strong sense of loyalty to and identification with his own people, the in-group. Through this socialization process, each member also acquires the belief that the culture of his own group, its values and goals, are the right and proper ones. So that almost inevitably, when two in-groups must face the problem of living together, each group considers the other an out-group and some degree of antagonism nearly always arises. In one of the most recent works on minorities in the United States, Charles F. Marden and Gladys Meyer contend that the immediate harmonious assimilation of two visibly different groups is impossible.[6] The fact is that ethnocentrism and in-group-out-group processes are well established universal sociological principles which characterize, at least, the initial stages of

---

[6]Charles F. Marden and Gladys Meyer, Minorities in American Society (New York: American Book Company, 1962) p. 36.

interaction between a dominant and minority group and, in instances of sustained cultural conflict, the continuing relations between the group. Ethnic identification may be used operationally as a rough index of "ethnic consciousness," but a more precise index is the objective index provided by a person's associations and adherence to ethnic attributes (attitudes and beliefs). The questions on the schedule were designed to provide an empirical description of ethnic consciousness in political behavior as well as an index of its dynamic character; always in the process of change. This is an essential feature of the problem. Ethnic consciousness is a phenomenon in process, related to specific events and long term currents. But ethnic consciousness as expressed in voting behavior is not exceedingly dynamic in character, although the stimuli which create behavior illustrative of ethnic consciousness may be, as in the case in this survey since it is related to specific events,[7] albeit within the context of long term currents.

Political stimuli. The interview schedules provide for the measurement of responses to external political stimuli which is defined here as (1) exposure to mass media (more specifically, to the Spanish television program, the Spanish-English newspaper, and religious and labor newspapers; (2) political speeches; (3) contacts by political party workers; and (4) political discussions in the family, and with friends and relatives (mutual influence of individuals within the

─────────────

[7]The May, 1963 mayoralty election in Denver, Colorado.

immediate social environment and (5) membership or identification with groups and associations with specific political orientation. Only exposure to selected mass media is treated in the statistical correlations.

Operational Definitions

The concepts were translated into sets of operations as follows: Both subjective and objective indicators of ethnic consciousness are used. Indices of an objective nature consist of (1) greater association with Spanish persons than with Anglos (2) attendance at "Spanish" churches, (3) speaking Spanish, belonging to Spanish organizations. Those of a subjective nature are provided by expressed beliefs and feelings relative to "being Spanish."

Exposure to selected mass media communication is measured by a battery of eleven questions included in the questionnaires used in the three interviews. Whether the respondent ever read the Spanish-English newspaper, listened to the Spanish language radio station, or viewed Spanish language television programs and to what degree he did any or all of these things was the determining factor in deciding the degree of exposure to this selected mass media (a Guttman scaling technique was used to determine the exact degree for each respondent).

Description of the Instruments

The basic instruments were a series of interview schedules consisting of questions to be answered by the respondents and filled in by the interviewer. The interview schedule used for the first pre-test

consisted of twenty-eight items, whereas the schedule for the first
actual pre-election survey consisted of thirty-three items or questions.
The second pre-election survey consisted of twenty items, and the post-
election schedule contained twelve items. The questions on the interview schedules were designed to render data appropriate for indices of
the phenomena to be studied and analyzed.

Schedule A: An instrument for securing social-economic and
identifying information on respondents and also the respondent's predispositions, attitudes, associations, exposure to various forms of
mass communication, and attitudes and positions specifically related to
candidates and issues in the 1963 Denver mayoralty election.

Schedule B: This schedule is an instrument for securing information on any changes occuring in the respondent's attitudes and reasons
therefor, exposure to mass communication, and changes in position relative to the mayoralty election, since the first interview.

Schedule C: This is the post-election interview schedule and is
the instrument for securing information regarding the final attitudes
and positions of the respondent relative to the candidates and how the
respondent finally expressed or failed to express his opinions and attitudes at the polls.

Techniques of Analysis

The procedure of an explanatory survey should yield reliable
evidence on the relationship of the phenomenon of voting behavior to one

or more independent variables or causes and thereby provide solutions to
the given problem of explanation.

Since the panel survey is only one part of a larger study of
political behavior and motivation of Hispano-Americans in southwestern
United States, the techniques of analysis herein discussed apply only to
the data secured by means of three different interviews with the same
respondents and therefore is limited to Hispano-Americans in the City
and County of Denver and applies to the specific situation brought about
by the May, 1962 election campaign and mayoralty election in Denver.

The data tabulated according to (1) identification statistics
or variables, (2) the quantitative ranges of the major concepts or independent variables: ethnicity and exposure to selected mass communication media, and (3) finally, as to relationships between variables.

Data relating to age, income, education, and other characteristics of the respondents are shown on histograms, Figures 5, 6, 7, 8, 9,
10, and 11. See Appendix J for coding instructions.

A Guttman scalogram method of scaling was used to obtain the
respondent's score expressing degree of ethnicity.[8] This same technique
was used to score degrees of exposure to selected mass media. A variation of the scalogram technique as devised by Guttman was used for

---

[8]Pauline V. Young, op. cit., pp. 336-341.

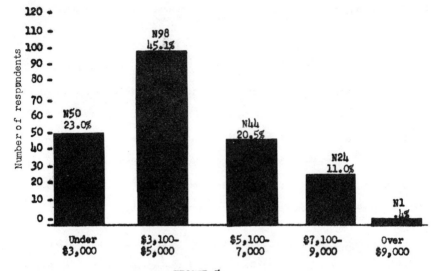

FIGURE 5

RESPONDENTS COUNTED AT DIFFERENT
INCOME LEVELS

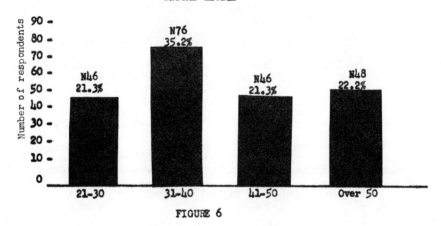

FIGURE 6

RESPONDENTS COUNTED AT DIFFERENT
AGE LEVELS

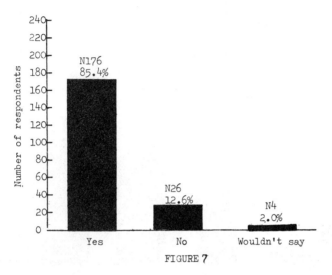

FIGURE 7

CHURCH MEMBERSHIP

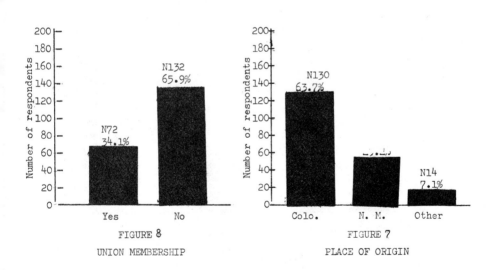

FIGURE 8

UNION MEMBERSHIP

FIGURE 7

PLACE OF ORIGIN

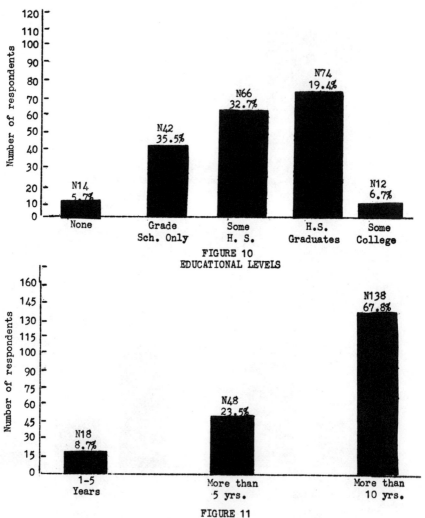

FIGURE 10
EDUCATIONAL LEVELS

FIGURE 11
LENGTH OF RESIDENCE IN DENVER

executing a "scale analysis" on items relating to the various degrees
of ethnicity and the different degrees of exposure to ethnic propaganda.
A scalogram board was constructed. By shifting rows and columns and by
eliminating whole rows an attempt was made to approach as closely as
possible an ideal scale. The rows that were eliminated represented
answers to questions 5d and 5f on ethnicity which were eliminated because there was no definite pattern to the responses to these questions.
Also, in executing a "scale analysis" on items relating to "exposure to
ethnic propaganda," questions 7d and 7e were eliminated in like manner.
The data then formed a scale approximating the ideal to the extent
that a conclusion was reached that the instruments used to measure ethnicity in one instance and exposure to ethnic propaganda in another
possessed unidimensionality.[9] The qualitative variables thus formed a
scale for the sample of Hispano respondents because they could be
arranged in a rank order on the scale score in a manner that was con-
sistent with their rank order on any or all of the variables and the coefficient of reproducibility of .93 for all of the combined scaled items
on ethnicity and .91 on "exposure" were well within the criterion for
stating that the particular variables formed scales for the defined population.[10]

---

[9]Claire Selltiz, et al, op. cit., page 349.

[10]Pauline V. Young, op. cit., page 339.

In the final analysis, the instrument used to measure degrees of ethnicity was made up of the following seven questions (listed in the order of decreasing degrees of "difficulty" in answering favorably to the question):

SCHEDULE A

Question 5c. Would you want your son or daughter to marry an Anglo?
Coefficient of Reproducibility - .90

Question 5h. Do you prefer your "own people" as friends and associates?
Coefficient of Reproducibility - .88

Question 5i. How about your friends, are they mostly Spanish, mostly Anglo or about even?
Coefficient of Reproducibility - .90

Question 5e. How important is it to be proud of being Spanish?
Coefficient of Reproducibility - .92

Question 5a. Is Spanish spoken in your home?
Coefficient of Reproducibility - .94

Question 5b. Do you want your children to learn and speak Spanish?
Coefficient of Reproducibility - .94

Question 5g. Do you belong to any "Spanish" organization or groups?
Coefficient of Reproducibility - .92

The instrument finally used to measure intensity of exposure to "ethnic propaganda" was made up of the following seven questions (also listed in order of decreasing degrees of "difficulty" in answering favorably):

SCHEDULE B

Question 4. During the past two weeks, can you recall seeing and hearing anything on "Festival Espanol" about the election or the candidates?
Coefficient of Reproducibility - .87

Question 3. During the past two weeks can you remember hearing anything
on the Spanish radio station about the election or the candidates?
Coefficient of Reproducibility - .90

Question 5. During the past two weeks did you see or read anything
about the election or the candidates in the Spanish newspaper, "El Tiempo"?
Coefficient of Reproducibility - .89

SCHEDULE A

Question 7b. How often do you listen to the Denver Spanish radio station?
Coefficient of Reproducibility - .89

Question 7c. How often do you watch the television program "Festival
Espanol"?
Coefficient of Reproducibility - .92

SCHEDULE B

Question 2. During the past two weeks can you recall reading anything
in the newspapers about the election or the candidates?
Coefficient of Reproducibility - .95

SCHEDULE A

Question 7d. How often do you read a church or religious newspaper or
magazine?
Coefficient of Reproducibility - .94

The number of possible responses to each question on the ethnicity instrument ranged from 3 to 4 categories of responses and on the
"exposure" instrument they also ranged from 3 to 4 categories of
responses. But in each case, they were arbitrarily dichotomized into
only two categories of responses (favorable or unfavorable, 0 or 1). A
total score was obtained for each person in the sample. Any person's
score on ethnicity was then based on the sum of the weights of his

responses to all the items which were included in the ethnicity scale and and any person's score on "exposure" on items included in the "exposure" scale. All of the respondents were then ranked from 0 to 7 degrees of ethnicity and 0 to 7 degrees of "exposure." Respondents who answered all seven questions in each of the scales in ways indicating high ethnicity and high "exposure," respectively are all lined up in solid black columns along the left section of the ethnicity or the "exposure" scalograms. See photographic reproductions in Figure 12. Those with progressively fewer "favorable" responses, scale lower and lower to the right of the scalogram. For each scale, the respondents were then arbitrarily divided into two categories: Those with 4 or more favorable or positive responses were designated as respondents with high ethnicity, and those with less than 4 favorable or positive responses as respondents with low ethnicity. The same procedure was used in setting up the two categories of respondents, those with high "exposure" and those with low "exposure" to ethnic propaganda.

The following is a more detailed explanation of the photographs of the scales used to rank the respondents as to degree of ethnicity and as to degree of exposure to Hispano oriented mass communication propaganda:

1. The numbers along the bottom rows identify the respondents as they rank along the scale. In the ethnicity scale, the ones to the extreme left are the most ethnically oriented. The degree of ethnicity diminishes gradually toward the extreme right where respondents with practically no ethnicity are found. In the "exposure to propaganda" sdale those at the extreme left were greatly exposed to this propaganda, the degree of exposure diminishing toward the extreme right

ETHNICITY SCALE

Breaking Points of Scale

Rows represent 7 questions

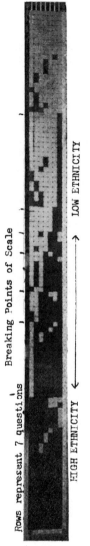

HIGH ETHNICITY ← → LOW ETHNICITY

Black blocks in columns represent "favorable" responses by respondents to each of 7 questions
White blocks represent "unfavorable" responses.

EXPOSURE INTENSITY SCALE

Breaking Points

Rows represent 7 questions

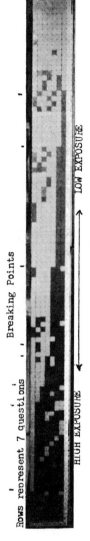

HIGH EXPOSURE ← → LOW EXPOSURE

Black blocks in columns represent "favorable" responses by respondents to each of 7 questions
White blocks represent "unfavorable" responses

FIGURE 12

SCALOGRAMS USED IN SCALING DEGREE OF ETHNICITY AND
DEGREE OF EXPOSURE TO ETHNIC ORIENTED PROPAGANDA

where respondents with practically no exposure to this type of propaganda are found.

2. The numbers along the left hand side vertical line identify the questions used in the interviews to measure ethnicity and exposure to ethnic oriented propaganda.

3. For the purposes of this study, four categories were arbitrarily established on the basis of the scale ranking, for the two variables, ethnicity and exposure. These were: respondents with high ethnicity, respondents with low ethnicity, respondents with high degree of exposure to ethnic propaganda and respondents with low degree of exposure to ethnic propaganda.

Procedure for handling data. For the panel survey, data secured through the three different interviews was coded in accordance with coding instructions prepared to classify data pertinent to the purpose of the survey. The data were then punched on IBM cards. Also punched on the IBM cards were the code numbers indicating the degree of ethnicity and exposure to selected mass media for each person in the survey. The degree of ethnicity and exposure had previously been established for each person by means of the Guttman scaling technique. The IBM cards were then sorted or counted according to the specified categories used in describing voting behavior and distributions presented in the various figures and tables referred to in the thesis.

Statistical tests. The McNemar test was used to test the significance of changes in choice of candidates in two related samples: (1) ethnically oriented respondents, (2) "others" or Anglo-oriented respondents. Due to small frequencies, the binomial test was used instead of the

McNemar to test the significance of changes in choice of candidates in two other related samples: (1) ethnically oriented respondents with high exposure to ethnic propaganda via mass communication media, (2) "others" or Anglo-oriented respondents with similar high exposure to ethnic propaganda.[11] The simple chi-square test was used to test the change toward greater interest and greater intention to vote in the election from the first to the second interview, (1) among the ethnically oriented respondents and (2) among the "others" or Anglo-oriented respondents, (3) among the ethnically oriented respondents with high exposure to ethnic propaganda, and (4) among the ethnically oriented respondents with low exposure to ethnic propaganda.[12] The Pearson product-moment coefficient of correlation was used to measure the co-relation between (1) ethnicity and age categories, (2) ethnicity and income categories, and (3) ethnicity and amount of education.[13]

The Findings

The numbers of changers and non-changers in the choice of candidates among ethnically oriented respondents are shown on a contingency table (see Table XVI) used in the application of the McNemar test for

---

[11] Sidney Siegâl, Nonparametric Statistics for the Behavioral Sciences (New York: McGraw-Hill Book Company, Inc., 1956), pp. 63-67.

[12] Pauline V. Young, Scientific Social Surveys and Research (third edition; Englewood Cliffs, New Jersey, 1956), p. 299.

[13] Ibid., pp. 285-293.

TABLE XVI

NUMBER OF CHANGERS AND NON-CHANGERS IN CHOICE
OF CANDIDATES AMONG ETHNICALLY
ORIENTED RESPONDENTS*

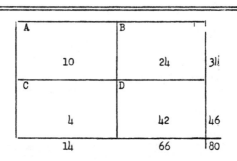

	A	B	
	10	24	34
C		D	
	4	42	46
	14	66	80

A - Currigan-Grant supporters and undecided
voters who went to Batterton

B - Currigan-Grant supporters who stayed with
Currigan-Grant

C - Batterton supporters who stayed with
Batterton

D - Batterton supporters and undecided who
went to Currigan-Grant

McNemar Test

$$\chi^2 = \frac{(A - D - 1)^2}{A + D} = 18.48$$

d.f. = 1

Significant at .01 level

*Shown on a 2 x 2 contingency table used in the applica-
tion of the McNemar test for significance of change.

significance of change. On the basis of this analysis, H_o was rejected and H_1 was accepted.

The numbers of changers and non-changers among <u>ethnically oriented respondents with high exposure to ethnic propaganda</u> are shown on a contingency table (see Table XVII) used in the application of the binomial test for significance of change. On the basis of this analysis, H_o was rejected and H_2 was accepted.

The number of changers and non-changers among "<u>others</u>" or <u>respondents with low ethnicity</u> are shown on a contingency table (see Table XVIII) used in the application of the McNemar Test for significance of change. On the basis of this analyses, H_o was accepted and H_3 was rejected.

The number of changers and non-changers among "<u>others</u>" with <u>high exposure to ethnic propaganda</u> are shown on a contingency table (see Table XIX) use in the application of the binomial test for significance of change. On the basis of this analyses, H_o was accepted and H_4 was rejected.

The number of <u>ethnically oriented respondents</u> who changed to greater interest in the election and the number of "<u>others</u>" who changed toward greater interest in the election are shown on Table XX used in the application of the Chi Square Test. On the basis of this analyses, H_o was rejected, H_5 was accepted.

Table XXI (a contingency table used in the application of the

TABLE XVII

NUMBER OF CHANGERS AND NON-CHANGERS IN CHOICE OF CANDIDATES
AMONG ETHNICALLY ORIENTED RESPONDENTS WITH HIGH
EXPOSURE TO ETHNICALLY ORIENTED PROPAGANDA*

	A	B	
	4	2	6
	C	D	
	2	20	22
	6	22	28

A - Currigan-Grant supporters and undecided
     voters who went to Batterton

B - Currigan-Grant supporters who stayed with
     Currigan-Grant

C - Batterton supporters who stayed with
     Batterton

D - Batterton supporters and undecided who
     went to Currigan-Grant

Binomial Test**

N = 24   x = 4

Significant at .05 level

*Shown on a 2 x 2 contingency table used in the application of
the Binomial Test.

**See Sidney Siegel, op. cit., page 67.

TABLE XVIII

NUMBER OF CHANGERS AND NON-CHANGERS IN CHOICE
OF CANDIDATES AMONG "OTHERS" OR
ANGLO-ORIENTED RESPONDENTS*

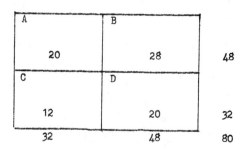

A 20	B 28	48
C 12	D 20	32
32	48	80

A - Currigan-Grant supporters and undecided
voters who went to Batterton

B - Currigan-Grant supporters who stayed with
Currigan-Grant

C - Batterton supporters who stayed with
Batterton

D - Batterton supporters and undecided who
went to Currigan-Grant

McNemar Test

$$x^2 = \frac{(A - D - 1)^2}{A+D} = .025$$
$$d.f. = 1$$

Not significant at .05 level

*Shown on a 2 x 2 contingency table used in the application of
the McNemar test for significance of change.

TABLE XIX

CHANGERS AND NON-CHANGERS IN CHOICE OF CANDIDATES AMONG "OTHERS"
OR ANGLO ORIENTED RESPONDENTS WITH HIGH EXPOSURE
TO ETHNICALLY ORIENTED PROPAGANDA*

A	B	
6	4	10
C	D	
8	12	20
14	16	30

A - Currigan-Grant supporters and undecided
    voters who went to Batterton

B - Currigan-Grant supporters who stayed with
    Currigan-Grant

C - Batterton supporters who stayed with
    Batterton

D - Batterton supporters and undecided who went
    to Currigan-Grant

Binomial Test**

n = 18   x = 6

Not significant at .05 level

*Shown on a 2 x 2 contingency table used in the application of
the Binomial Test.

**See Sidney Siegel, op. cit., page 67.

TABLE XX

CHANGE TOWARD GREATER INTEREST IN ELECTION,
FIRST TO SECOND INTERVIEWS*

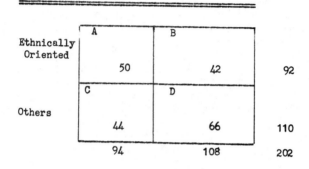

	A	B	
Ethnically Oriented	50	42	92
Others	C	D	
	44	66	110
	94	108	202

Chi Square Test

$$\chi^2 = \frac{N\left(AD - BC - \frac{N}{2}\right)2}{(A\ B)\ (C\ D)\ (A\ C)\ (B\ D)} = 3.58**$$

d.f. = 1

Significant at .05 level.

*Numbers shown on a 2 x 2 contingency table for use in applying the χ^2 test to determine if the observed breakdown of frequencies could have occurred under H_0.

**Incorporates a correction for continuity, see Sidney Siegel, op. cit., p. 107.

TABLE XXI

CHANGE TOWARD GREATER INTENTION TO VOTE
DURING ELECTION CAMPAIGN*

	Change	No Change	
Ethnically Oriented	24	66	90
Other	22	88	110
	46	154	200

<u>Chi Square Test</u>

$$\chi^2 = \frac{N(\mid AD - BC \mid - \frac{N}{2})^2}{(A\ B)\ (C\ D)\ (A+C\ (B+D)} = .89$$

d.f. = 1

Not significant at .05 level

*Numbers shown on a 2 x 2 contingency table for use in applying the χ^2 test to determine if the observed breakdown of frequencies could have occurred under H_o.

Chi Square Test) shows the number of <u>ethnically</u> <u>oriented</u> <u>respondents</u> who changed toward greater intention to vote in the election as compared to the number of "<u>others</u>" who changed toward greater intention to vote in the election. On the basis of this analysis shown in the table, H_0 was sustained and H_6 was rejected.

Table XXII (a contingency table used in the application of the Chi Square Test) shows the number of <u>ethnically</u> <u>oriented</u> <u>respondents</u> <u>with</u> <u>high</u> <u>exposure</u> <u>to</u> <u>ethnic</u> <u>propaganda</u> who changed toward greater interest in the election from the first to the second interview as compared with "<u>others</u>" <u>with</u> <u>high</u> <u>exposure</u> <u>to</u> <u>ethnic</u> <u>propaganda</u> who changed toward greater interest in the election. On the basis of this analysis, H_0 was sustained, and H_7 was rejected.

Table XXIII (a contingency table used in the application of the Chi Square Test) shows the number of <u>ethnically</u> <u>oriented</u> <u>respondents</u> <u>with</u> <u>high</u> <u>exposure</u> <u>to</u> <u>ethnic</u> <u>propaganda</u> who changed toward greater intention to vote in the election from the first to the second interview as compared to the number of "<u>others</u>" <u>with</u> <u>high</u> <u>exposure</u> who changed to greater intention to vote in the election from the first to the second interview. On the basis of this analysis, H_0 was rejected, and H_8 was accepted.

Table XXIV is a correlation table used in computing the Pearsonian coefficient of correlation between degrees of ethnicity and different levels of education among the respondents. On the basis of the computations, there does not appear to be either a positive or negative correla-

TABLE XXII

CHANGE TOWARD GREATER INTEREST IN ELECTION
FIRST TO SECOND INTERVIEWS*

	Change	No Change	
Ethnically oriented with high exposure to selected mass media	20	18	38
Others with high exposure to selected mass media	18	18	36

<u>Chi Square Test</u>

$$\chi^2 = \frac{N(\ AD - BC\ \frac{N}{2}\ )^2}{(A+B)(C+D)(A+C)(B+D)} = .0001$$

d.f. = 1

Not significant at .05 level

*Numbers shown on a 2 x 2 contingency table for use in applying the χ^2 test to determine if the observed breakdown of frequencies could have occurred under H_o.

TABLE XXIII

CHANGE TO GREATER INTENTION TO VOTE
DURING ELECTION CAMPAIGN*

Others with high exposure to selected mass media	A 8	B 30	38
Ethnically oriented with high exposure to selected mass media	C 20	D 16	36
	28	46	74

Chi Square Test

$$\chi^2 = \frac{N(AD - BC - \frac{N}{2})^2}{(A+B)\ (C+D)\ (A+C)\ (B+D)} = 7.94$$

d.f. = 1

Significant at .01 level

*Numbers shown on a 2 x 2 contingency table for use in applying the χ^2 test to determine if the observed breakdown of frequencies could have occurred under H_o.

TABLE XXIV

CORRELATION TABLE

ETHNICITY RATE	EDUCATION CATEGORIES						
	TOTAL	NONE	GRADE SCHOOL	HIGH SCHOOL	HIGH SCH. GRAD.	SOME COLLEGE	COLLEGE GRAD.
7	38	10	12	16	0	0	0
6	30	4	18	6	2	0	0
5	8	0	4	4	0	0	0
4	44	0	2	18	24	0	0
3	19	0	1	4	8	6	0
2	10	0	4	6	0	0	0
1	39	0	0	12	24	2	1
0	20	0	0	0	16	4	0
TOTALS	208	14	41	66	74	12	1

$$Y = \frac{\frac{-348}{208} - (-.26) \times .154}{2.39 \times 1.035} = -.0879$$

Using the Pearson Product-Moment
Coefficient of Correlation,
the correlation
between different degrees of ethnicity
and different levels of education
is not significant at the .05 level.

tion that is statistically significant at the .05 level.

Table XXV is a correlation table used in computing the Pearsonian coefficient of correlation between degrees of ethnicity and different income categories. On the basis of these computations, there does not appear to be either a positive or negative correlation that is statistically significant at the .05 level.

Table XXVI is a correlation table used in computing the Pearsonian coefficient of correlation between degrees of ethnicity and different age categories. On the basis of these computations, there does not appear to be either a positive or negative correlation that is statistically significant at the .05 level.

TABLE XXV

CORRELATION TABLE

Ethnicity Rank	INCOME CATEGORIES					
	Total	Less than $3,000	$3,000-5,000	$5,100-7,000	$7,100-9,000	Over $9,000
7	50	14	30	4	2	0
6	30	12	10	6	2	0
5	10	2	4	2	2	0
4	16	4	6	4	2	0
3	26	2	10	10	4	0
2	16	2	4	4	6	0
1	22	4	8	8	2	0
0	47	10	26	6	4	1
Total	217	50	98	44	24	1

$$V = \frac{\frac{114}{217} - (-.424) \times .207}{2.698 \times .934} = -.0780$$

Using the Pearson Product-Moment
Coefficient of Correlation,
the correlation
between different degrees of ethnicity
and different income categories.
is not significant at the .05 level.

TABLE XXVI

CORRELATION TABLE

Ethnicity High to Low Rank	AGE CATEGORIES				
	Total	20-29	30-39	40-49	Over 50
7	54	2	20	20	12
6	30	4	14	2	10
5	10	4	0	4	2
4	18	6	6	2	4
3	10	8	0	2	0
2	10	0	8	2	0
1	40	8	16	6	10
0	44	14	12	8	10
Total	216	46	76	46	48

$$\gamma = \frac{\frac{58}{216} - (-.435) \times .466}{2.792 \times 1.046} = .112$$

Using the Pearson Product-Moment
Coefficient of Correlation,
the correlation
between different degrees of ethnicity
and different age categories
is not significant at the .05 level.

CHAPTER VIII

THE MACROSCOPIC VIEW

Summary of Research Findings

The main objective of the panel survey portion of this thesis was
to determine if ethnicity alone or in combination with exposure to selected mass media communication had any significant relation to the amount
of interest, intention to vote, and choice of candidates in a municipal
election. The following differences in the choice of candidates, change
in amount of interest, and change in intention to vote were found in comparing different groups, (1) Spanish oriented, (2) Anglo oriented, (3)
Spanish oriented with high exposure, and (4) Anglo oriented with high exposure: The proportion of voter-respondents in the Hispano oriented group
who changed or took a position (from an undecided status) in favor of
Currigan-Grant was significantly greater than those who changed or took
a position for Batterton.[1]

But there was no significant difference among Anglo oriented
(other) voter-respondents in the proportion who changed or took a position
in favor of Currigan-Grant and those who changed or took a position in
favor of Batterton. The above held true when another independent variable, exposure to selected mass media communication was introduced. Exposure to selected mass media communication made no difference among Anglo
oriented voter-respondents.

_____

[1]Considered by most Hispano opinion leaders and the Hispano public generally as anti-Hispano.

In analyzing the data for any significant difference in the increase in interest in the election as the campaign progressed, it was found
that there was a significantly greater proportion of Spanish oriented respondents who changed from the no interest to interest category than
among Anglo oriented respondents. However, when only Spanish oriented
and Anglo oriented respondents who had had high exposure to mass media
communication were compared in respect to change toward greater interest
in the election, no significant difference was found.

With respect to change toward greater intention to vote, there
was a significant difference between Spanish oriented respondents with
high exposure and Anglo oriented respondents with high exposure but no
significant difference when comparing Spanish oriented and Anglo oriented
respondents and leaving out the exposure variable. There is no doubt,
on the basis of the statistical analysis that ethnic oriented voter-
respondents, whether they were highly exposed to mass media communication
or not, tended to vote in larger proportion for candidates generally believed acceptable to the Hispano group than non-ethnic or Anglo oriented
voter-respondents.

This was also true with reference to changes toward greater interest in the election, but held only when the total number of ethnic
oriented and non-ethnic oriented were combined and not when only those
with high exposure in both groups were tested together. In other words,
both groups changed equally when more highly exposed to mass media communication.

There is no such clear-cut and significant difference when changes toward greater intention to vote are measured if the exposure variable is eliminated. But when Spanish and Anglo oriented respondents (both equally highly exposed to mass media communication) are compared, the number of Hispano oriented respondents whose intention to vote increased is significantly greater than the number of Anglo oriented respondents. For the purposes of this study, the important finding is the positive relationship between ethnicity and voting behavior.

Interpretation and Implications

But a correlation between the fact of being an Hispano, a Negro, or a Jew and voting in a certain way is interestingly informative but still information pitched at a low level of abstraction. Generalizations of this type have a tendency to become, over a sufficient period of time, rather useless if not reformulated in more general terms.

Hispanos in pre-depression days before the 1930's favored the Republican Party. In the 1930's this relationship was reversed and it is plausible that the relationship could again reverse itself. Yet there must be more reliable "laws" of social behavior or political behavior of ethnic and racial groups. We must assume such laws to exist. There should be sociological propositions that would enable us to anticipate the circumstances under which the Hispano (or the Negro or Jewish) vote will grow more or less distinctive or what other populations or population groups might be expected to react in the same way to a set of given circumstances.

It is, of course, necessary to establish empirically whether a positive and important relationship does in fact exist between ethnicity or the "racial urge" and voting behavior. We believe this has been established for Hispanos in a given election in a given geographical area. We have also shown, we believe, that there is at the present time in various parts of the United States Southwest an increase in ethnicity among the Hispanos and that it can and does translate itself into effective political behavior. But this is not enough. It is also necessary to know under what circumstances this ethnicity or "racial urge" rises or falls, and it is equally important to discover and take into account all factors which mediate between ethnicity and voting behavior. To formulate sociological propositions that will not become obsolete or period pieces over a period of time, it is necessary systematically to discover, measure, and account for social, psychological, economic, and political factors which mediate the relationship between ethnicity and voting behavior, as well as to measure and account for these factors in the conditions that lie between ethnicity and party and candidate choice or position on political issues.

The study of attitudes, as a technique, represents an approach that maximizes explanatory power while dealing with a minimum number of variables. It provides a mode of explanation with roots in the "field theory." While mechanical laws connect two widely separated events, in field theory, the field "at the moment" is seen as a product of the field in the immediate neighborhood at a time just past. The initial

measurements are at the cross sections of a funnel that lie very close
to the dependent event (voting in our case), with "historical" explana-
tions proceeding backward in short steps. This is precisely the mode
of explanation we attempt here.

In other words, the use of attitudes to explain voting behavior
revolves around a proximal mode of explanation. Whatever effect distant
events (personal or otherwise) may have on current political behavior,
this effect is measurable just prior to the event in some form (ethnicity) using subjective and objective measures of ethnicity as in the
present study.

The field theory makes it possible to measure a person's political behavior at a current time on the basis of events in the individual's life history as well as in the events in the life history of his
group. Although the interviews in the panel survey give us data close
(in point of time) to the dependent behavior, the data tops other factors dating back into the past. This idea might be represented in the
form of a funnel in the manner shown on Figure 13.

Similarly, the "time span" represented by the funnel might be
reversed to predict the voting behavior of a group, ethnically or
racially differentiated, on the basis of attitudes and voting behavior
which are measured "at the moment," as shown in Figure 14.

If it is possible to establish combinations of factors or conditions under which the "racial" urge rises and falls, one should be able

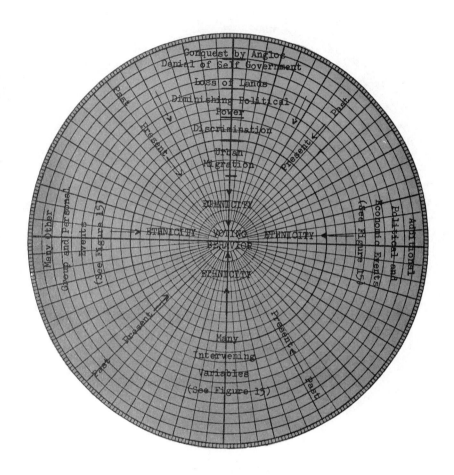

FIGURE 13

LIFE HISTORY OF A GROUP AND ITS RELATION
TO ETHNICITY AND VOTING BEHAVIOR

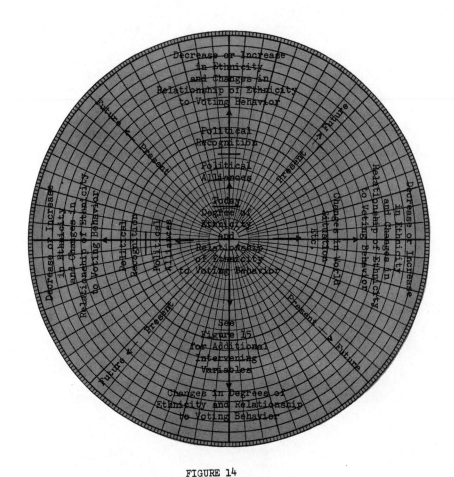

FIGURE 14

PREDICTING VOTING BEHAVIOR
IN TERMS OF ETHNICITY

to set forth the circumstances under which ethnicity will become an important factor in the voting behavior of members of racial, ethnic, or religious groups. A suggested model for use in accomplishing this is found in Figures 15 and 16.

It is not within the scope of this dissertation further to develop concepts and methods necessary for determining regularities in the functional relationship of cultural and behavioral patterns. It was important, however, to distinguish a scientific, generalizing approach from a historical, particularizing approach to the problem with which this thesis has been concerned and to suggest ways to move from microscopic to macroscopic considerations and implications.

Unlike certain aspects of modern culture (e.g., systems of money, banking, and credit), voting behavior cannot be studied apart from individual behavior. But voting (and its consequences) in a modern and complex socio-cultural system is an extremely heterogeneous entity, consisting of many interrelated parts. This complexity and heterogeneity is considerably reduced when the phenomenon of voting is studied and analyzed by sub-cultures or contracultures, since members of these subsocieties share a more substantial core of behavior.

But it would be the height of naivete to assume that these members are not subjected to numerous cross-pressures and influenced by multi-group association. They are members of a subculture, but they also participate in special portions of the entire culture. The voting

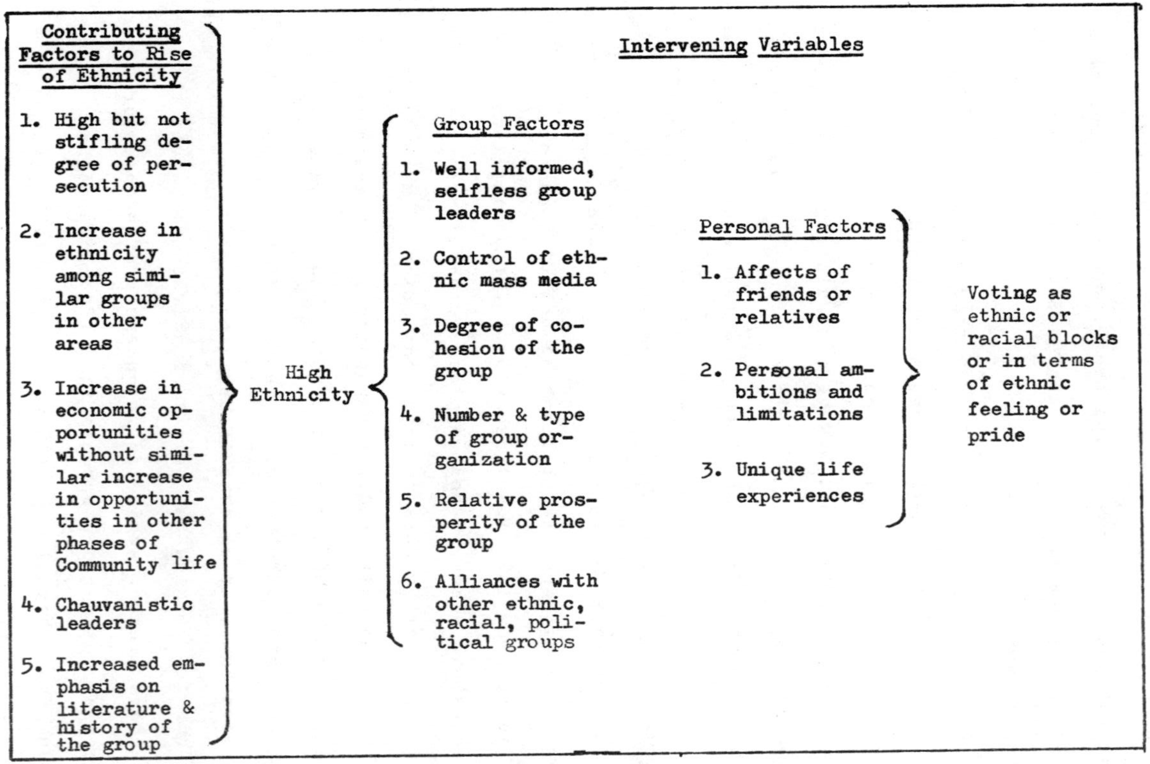

Intervening Variables

Contributing Factors to Rise of Ethnicity

1. High but not stifling degree of persecution

2. Increase in ethnicity among similar groups in other areas

3. Increase in economic opportunities without similar increase in opportunities in other phases of Community life

4. Chauvanistic leaders

5. Increased emphasis on literature & history of the group

High Ethnicity

Group Factors

1. Well informed, selfless group leaders

2. Control of ethnic mass media

3. Degree of cohesion of the group

4. Number & type of group organization

5. Relative prosperity of the group

6. Alliances with other ethnic, racial, political groups

Personal Factors

1. Affects of friends or relatives

2. Personal ambitions and limitations

3. Unique life experiences

Voting as ethnic or racial blocks or in terms of ethnic feeling or pride

FIGURE 15

CORE OF FUNNEL

Factors Contributing to Fall of Ethnicity or the "Racial Urge"

1. Fast spaced integration of the mass of the ethnic or racial group

2. Loss of language, religious, and other important culture traits

3. Geographical dispersal of the ethnic or racial group

4. Stifling suppression or persecution

5. Economic opportunities with corresponding social and political opportunities

Low Ethnicity

Intervening Variables

Social, Economic, and Group Factors

1. Highly organized minority within the minority

2. Exploitation by other groups

3. Entangling alliances

Personal Factors

1. Unique life experiences

2. Personal limitations and ambitions

Voting Behavior

Greater similarity to voting behavior of the general population, expressed through economic, religious, or several organizations or interests, or on the basis of political affiliation or economic class.

FIGURE 15 (Continued)

behavior of any ethnic or racial group must be analyzed in terms of
many subcultures. Membership in unions, trade associations, religious
organizations, and similar groups must be taken into account not only
in explaining present voting behavior but in predicting it.

An individual reacts as a total person in his functions, whether
as a member of the family, his community, his nation, or his ethnic
group. This, however, should not deter us from the search for valid
laws or regularities in the behavior of human beings. The first step
in the search is to establish regularities in the subcultures which
characterize modern sociocultural systems.

The next step is, perhaps, even more difficult. Although
national patterns or institutions and the subcultural segments are distinguishable and must be treated separately, they are so interdependent
functionally that neither can be understood properly unless related to
each other.

SELECTED BIBLIOGRAPHY

A. BOOKS

Ackoff, Russell L. The Design of Social Research. Chicago: University
of Chicago Press, 1953.

Barreiro, Antonio. Ojeada Sobre Nuevo Mejico. Puebla, Mexico: Imprenta
Jose M. Campos, 1832.

Barron, Milton. American Minorities. New York: Alfred A. Knopf, 1957.

Bean, Louis H. How to Predict Elections. New York: Alfred A. Knopf,
Inc., 1948.

Beck, Warren A. New Mexico: A History of Four Centuries. Norman,
Oklahoma: University of Oklahoma Press, 1962.

Berelson, Bernard, Paul F. Lazarsfeld, and William M. McPhee. Voting.
Chicago: University of Chicago Press, 1954.

Bryson, Tyman, et al., (eds.) Approaches to National Unity. New York:
Harper and Brothers, 1945.

Burdick, Eugene and Arthur T. Brodbeck (eds.). American Voting
Behavior. Glencoe, Illinois: The Free Press, 1954.

Burma, John H. Spanish Speaking Groups in the United States. Durham:
Duke University Press, 1954.

Campbell, Angus, et al. The American Voter. Survey Research Center,
University of Michigan. New York: John Wiley & Sons, Inc., 1960.

Campbell, Angus and Homer C. Cooper. Group Differences in Attitudes
and Votes. A study of the 1954 Congressional Election. Survey
Research Center, Institute for Social Research, University of
Michigan. Ann Arbor, 1956.

Campbell, Angus, et al. The Voter Decides. Survey Research Center,
University of Michigan. Evanston, Illinois: Row, Peterson and
Company, 1954.

Collins, Adrian (trans.) The Inequality of Human Races. New York:
G.P. Putnam's Sons, 1915.

Commons, John R. The Economics of Collective Action. New York:
The MacMillan Company, 1950.

Darwin, Charles. The Origin of Species. New York: D. Appleton and Company, 1897.

Davies, Walter W.W. Gringo. Santa Fe: The Rydal Press, 1938.

Dollard, John. Caste and Class in a Southern Town. Second edition. New York: Harper and Brothers, 1949.

Donnelly, Thomas C. Government of New Mexico. Albuquerque: University of New Mexico Press, 1947.

Edmundson, Munro S., Los Manitos: A Study of Institutional Values. Middle American Research Institute, Tulane University. New Orleans, 1957.

Frazier, E. Franklin. Race and Culture Contacts in the Modern World. New York: Alfred A. Knopf, 1957.

Giddings, F.W. Principles of Sociology. New York: The MacMillan Company, 1896.

Goode, William J. and Paul K. Hatt. Methods in Social Research. New York: McGraw-Hill Book Company, Inc., 1952.

Gordon, Milton M. Assimilation in American Life. New York: Oxford University Press, 1964.

Gosnell, H.F. Grass Roots Politics. American Council on Public Affairs. Washington D.C., 1942.

Gregg, Josiah. Commerce of the Prairies. Philadelphia: J.B. Lippincott Company, 1962.

Gross, Llewellyn (ed.), Symposium on Sociological Theory. Evanston, Illinois: Row, Peterson, and Company, 1959.

Handlin, Oscar. The Uprooted. Boston: Little, Brown and Company, 1951.

Herskovits, Melville J. Acculturation: The Study of Culture Contact. Glouchester Massachusetts: Peter Smith, 1958.

Hofstadter, Richard. Social Darwinism in American Thought. Revised edition. Boston: The Beacon Press, 1955.

Hyman, Herbert. Political Socialization: A Study in the Psychology of Political Behavior. Glencoe, Illinois: The Free Press, 1959.

_____ Survey Design and Analysis. Glencoe, Illinois: The Free Press, 1955.

Jaszi, Oscar. Dissolution of the Hapsburg Monarchy. Chicago:
Phoenix Paperback #70, University of Chicago Press, 1957.

Jahoda, Marie, et al. Research Methods in Social Research.
Vol. I. New York: The Dryden Press, 1951.

Jonas, Frank H. (ed.). Western Politics and the 1956 Elections.
Salt Lake City: Institute of Government, University of Utah
Press, 1957.

Kenehan, Katherine. Colorado - The Land and the People. Denver
Public Schools, (Denver Public Schools Printing, 1957).

Kornhauser, Arthur (ed.). Problems of Power in American Society.
Fort Wayne, Indiana: Wayne University Press, 1957.

Lazarsfeld, Paul F., Bernard Berelson, and Hazel Gaudet. The
People's Choice. New York: Columbia University Press, 1944.

Lipset, Seymour Martin. Political Man. Garden City, New York:
Doubleday and Company, Inc., 1960.

Loomis, Charles P. Social Systems. Princeton: D. Von Nostrand
Company, 1960.

Loyola, Sister Mary. The American Occupation. Albuquerque:
University of New Mexico Press, 1939.

Mack, Raymond W. Race, Class and Power. New York: American Book
Company, 1964.

Madariaga, Salvador De. Englishmen, Frenchmen, Spaniards. London:
Oxford University Press, 1928.

Marden, Charles F. and Gladys Meyer. Minorities in American Society.
New York: American Book Company, 1962.

Martin, Curtis. Colorado Politics. Denver: Big Mountain Press,
1962.

Martindale, Don. Nature and Types of Sociological Theory. Boston:
Houghton Mifflin Company, 1960.

McCormick, Thomas C. and Roy G. Francis. Methods of Research in the
Behavioral Sciences. New York: Harper and Brothers, 1958.

McIver, R.M. The Web of Government. New York: The MacMillan
Company, 1947.

McPhee, William N. and William Glaser (eds.). Public Opinion and Congressional Elections. New York: Free Press of Glencoe, The MacMillan Company, 1962.

McWilliams, Carey. North from Mexico. Philadelphia and New York: J.B. Lippincott Company, 1949.

Mead, Margaret (ed.). Cultural Patterns and Technical Change. New York: The New American Library of World Literature, Inc., 1955.

Merriam, Charles Edward. Political Power. New York and London: McGraw-Hill Book Company, Inc., 1934.

Merton, Robert K. Social Theory and Social Structure. Glencoe Illinois: The Free Press, 1961.

Merton, Robert K. Social Theory and Social Structure. Revised edition. Glencoe, Illinois: The Free Press, 1957.

Merton, Robert K., Leonard Broom, and Leonard S. Cottrell (eds.). Sociology Today. New York: Basic Books, Inc., 1959.

Moore, F.W. (trans.) Outlines of Sociology. Philadelphia: American Academy of Political and Social Sciences, 1899.

Myrdal, Gunnar. An American Dilemma. New York and London: Harper and Brothers, 1944.

Otero, Miguel A. My Life on the Frontier. Albuquerque: University of New Mexico Press, 1937.

Park, Robert E. Race and Culture. Glencoe Illinois: The Free Press, 1950.

Park, R.E. and E.W. Burgess. Introduction to the Science of Sociology. Second edition. Chicago: University of Chicago Press, 1924.

Parsons, Talcott. Essays in Sociological Theory. Revised edition. Glencoe, Illinois: The Free Press, 1954.

_____. The Social System. Glencoe, Illinois: The Free Press, 1951.

Parten, Mildred. Surveys, Polls, and Samples: Practical Procedures. New York: Harper and Brothers, 1950.

Pino, Pedro Bautista. Exposicion Sucinta y Sencilla de la Provincia de Nuevo Mexico. Mexico D.F.: Imprenta de Lara, 1849.

Powell, Norman John. Anatomy of Public Opinion. Englewood Cliffs, New Jersey: Prentice-Hall, Inc., 1951.

Prince, Le Baron B. A Concise History of New Mexico. Cedar Rapids, Iowa: The Torch Press, 1914.

Rose, Arnold M. (ed.). The Institutions of Advanced Societies. Minneapolis: University of Minnesota Press, 1958.

Selltiz, Claire, et al. Research Methods in Social Relations. Revised one-volume edition. (Place of publication not given). Holt, Rinehart and Winston, 1961.

Siegel, Sidney. Nonparametric Statistics: for the Behavioral Sciences. New York: McGraw-Hill Book Company, Inc., 1956.

Simpson, George Eaton and J. Milton Yinger. Racial and Cultural Minorities. Revised edition. New York: Harper and Brothers, 1958.

Smith, Adam. The Theory of Moral Sentiments. New York: G.P. Putman's Sons, 1904.

Sorokin, Pitirim A. Society, Culture and Personality. New York and London: Harper and Brothers, 1947.

Spencer, Herbert. The Principles of Sociology. New York: D. Appleton, 1897.

Steward, Julian H. Theory of Culture Change. Urbana, Illinois: University of Illinois Press, 1955.

Stouffer, Samuel A. Social Research to Test Ideas. Glencoe, Illinois: The Free Press, 1962.

Stouffer, Samuel A., et al. Measurement and Prediction. Princeton: Princeton University Press, 1950.

_____. The American Soldier: Adjustment During Army Life. Princeton University Press, 1949.

Sumner, William Graham. Folkways. Boston: Ginn and Co., 1906.

Swanson, G.E., et al. (eds.). Readings in Social Psychology. New York: Henry Holt and Company, 1952.

Teggart, Frederick F. Theory and Processes of History. Berkeley and Los Angeles: University of California Press, 1960.

Timasheff, Nocolas S. _Sociological Theory_. Revised edition.
New York: Random House, 1957.

Tocqueville, Alexis de. _Democracy in America_. Vol. 1. New York:
Vintage Books, 1954.

Trujillo, Josue. _La Penitencia a Traves de la Civilizacion_.
(Pamphlet) Santa Fe Press, 1957. May be purchased by
writing _The Santa Fe New Mexican_, Santa Fe, New Mexico.

Twitchell, Ralph Emerson. _The Leading Facts of New Mexico History_.
Cedar Rapids, Iowa: Torch Press, 1911.

Valdes, Daniel T. (ed.). _Who's Who in Colorado_. Denver: Sage
Books, Inc., 1958.

Wallis, W. Allen, and Harry V. Roberts. _Statistics: A New
Approach_. Glencoe, Illinois: The Free Press, 1956.

Walter, Paul A.F., Jr. _Race and Culture Relations_. New York
and London: McGraw-Hill Book Company, Inc., 1956.

Warren, Roland L. _Studying Your Community_. New York: Russell
Sage Foundation, 1955.

Young, Kimball and Raymond W. Mack. _Sociology and Social Life_.
Second edition. New York: American Book Co., 1962.

Young, Pauline V. _Scientific Social Surveys and Research_.
Englewood Cliffs, New York: Prentice-Hall, Inc., 1956.

Zetterberg, Hans L. _On Theory and Verification in Sociology_.
New York: The Tressler Press, 1954.

B. PERIODICALS

Berelson, Bernard. "The Structure of Political Beliefs,"
Public Opinion Quarterly, XVI (1959), 313-330.

Blumer, Herbert. "Public Opinion and Public Opinion Polling,"
American Sociological Review, XIII (October, 1948), Bobs-
Merrill Reprint Series in the Social Sciences #32, pp. 542-554.

Broom, Leonard and John Kitsuse. "The Validation of Acculturation,"
American Anthropologist, LVII (February, 1955), p. 44.

Cantril, Hadley. "The Intensity of an Attitude," _Journal of
Abnormal and Social Psychology_, XLIV (1946), 129-135.

Cavan, R.S. "The Questionnaire in a Social Research Project,"
American Journal of Sociology, XXXVIII (1933), 721-727. .

Crawford, W. Rex. "The Latin American in Wartime U.S.," The
Annals of the American Academy of Political and Social Science,
(September, 1942), 123.

Duncan, Otis Dudley and Leo F. Schnore. "Cultural, Behavioral,
and Ecological Perspectives in the Study of Social Organizations," American Journal of Sociology, LXV (September, 1959),
Bobs-Merrill Reprint Series in the Social Sciences #75, pp. 132-146.

Eisenstadt, S.N. "The Process of Absorption of New Immigrants to
Israel," Human Relations, V (1952), 157-189.

Etzioni, Amitai. "The Ghetto-A Re-evaluation," Social Forces,
XXXVII (March, 1959), 255ff.

Glantz, Oscar. "Class Consciousness and Political Solidarity,"
American Sociological Review, XXIII, No. 4 (August, 1958), 375.

Glasser, William A. "Intention and Voting Turnout," American
Political Science Review, LII, No. 1 (December, 1958), 103.

Gordon, R. "Interaction Between Attitude and the Definition of
the Situation," American Sociological Review, XVII (1952),
50-58.

Lazarsfeld, Paul F. "The Use of Panels in Social Research,"
American Philosophical Society Proceedings (1945), 405-410.

Lazarsfeld, Paul F. and Marione Fiske. "The Panel as a New Tool
for Measuring Public Opinion," Public Opinion Quarterly
(February, 1938), 596-612.

Leites, Nathan. "Psycho-Cultural Hypotheses About Political
Acts," World Politics, I (October, 1948), 1.

Lipset, Seymour Martin. "Changing Social Status and Prejudice,"
Social Problems, VI (Winter, 1958, 1959) 253ff.

Lundberg, George A. "Some Neglected Aspects of the Minorities'
Problem," Modern Age, 2 (Summer, 1958) 290-291.

Malinowski, Bronislaw. "The Group and the Individual in Functional
Analysis," American Journal of Sociology, XLIV (May, 1939),
131-135.

Miyomato, S. Frank. "The Impact of Research on Different Conceptions
of Role," Sociological Inquiry (Spring, 1963), 114.

Riesman, David, "Tocqueville As Ethnographer," American Scholar, (Spring, 1961), 174.

Simmel, Georg. "Superiority and Subordination," American Journal of Sociology, II (September, 1896), 394-415.

Smith, Carl O. and Stephen O. Sarasohn. "Hate Propaganda in Detroit," Public Opinion Quarterly, X (1946), 24-52.

Smith, Joel, et al. "Communication and the Consequences of Communication," Sociological Inquiry, (Winter, 1962), 3.

Smith, M. Brewster. "Opinions, Personality and Political Behavior," The American Political Science Review, LII, No. 1 (March, 1958), 1.

Turner, Ralph H. "Role-Taking, Role Standpoint, and Reference Group Behavior," American Journal of Sociology, LXI (1956), 316-328.

Watson, John B., and Julian Samora. "Leadership in a Southwestern Community," American Sociological Review, XIX, No. 4 (August, 1954), 413-414.

Winthrop, Henry. "Political Innovation in Social Complexity," Sociological Inquiry, 78.

Wirth, Louis. "Consensus and Mass Communication," American Sociological Review, XIII (February, 1948) 1-15.

_____. "Types of Nationalism," American Journal of Sociology, XLI (May, 1936), 37-49.

C. GOVERNMENT PUBLICATIONS
PUBLIC DOCUMENTS

Denver Police Department. Annual Report. Denver: City and County of Denver, 1960.

Denver Housing Authority. Annual Report. Denver: City and County of Denver, 1961.

Denver Planning Office. Population Report. Bulletin R-2. Denver: City and County of Denver, 1962.

Denver Mayor's Commission on Human Relations. Denver Inventory of Human Relations. Denver: City and County of Denver, 1955.

Denver School Board. School Statistics. Denver: City and County of Denver, 1962.

Secretary of State. New Mexico Blue Book. Santa Fe: State of New
     Mexico, 1952.

                      D. UNPUBLISHED MATERIALS

Meier, Harold C. "Three Ethnic Groups in a Southwestern Community,"
     Unpublished Master's Thesis, University of Colorado, Boulder,
     1955.

Pfaff, Richard H. "The Effective Political Units in a Transitional
     Society," University of Colorado, 1951. (Mimeographed.)

Rendon, Gabino. "Voting Behavior in a Tri-Ethnic Community,"
     Unpublished Master's thesis, University of Colorado, Boulder,
     1962.

Valdes, Daniel T. "Spanish Speaking People of the Southwest," Colorado
     State Department of Education, 1938. (Mimeographed.)

_____. "Religious Preference and Voting Behavior in Denver in the
     1960 Presidential Election," unpublished seminar paper, University
     of Colorado, 1961.

APPENDIXES

EL TIEMPO

VOL. 1 — NO. 42

DENVER, COLORADO

Thursday, April 18, 1963

MEX-AMERICANS REVOLT IN TEXAS

DEFEAT ALL ANGLOS IN CITY ELECTION

In a dramatic revolt last week led by PASSO (Political Association of Spanish-Speaking Organizations) Mexican-Americans in the south Texas town of Crystal City captured all five seats on the city council, giving them control of the town government with authority to appoint the mayor, the marshall and other officers.

Although the Mexican-Americans out number the Anglo-Americans four to one in Crystal City, they had never even had a candidate run for any town office until this city was chosen by PASSO as a practical test of an all-out Mexican-American vote drive. Before the Anglo-Americans were aware of what was going on, twice as many Mexican-Americans as Anglos (1,139 to 532) had paid their poll taxes and had registered a vote. And when election time came last week, nearly every Mexican-American had turned out to vote and all had voted for Mexican-American candidates and for the first time in its history, the Anglo-Americans were no longer running the city.

*****

Albert Fuentes who led the campaign for PASSO is quoted as saying that the Mexican-Americans had done the "impossible" and that if it can be done in Crystal City it can be done all over Texas. He says, that on election day, the "Mexicans" have learned that all South Texans are equal.

CITY AND COUNTY OF DENVER

ELECTION RETURN

TITLE: GENERAL ELECTION

DATE: NOV. 6, 1962

SEC

PRECINCT	TOTAL PRECINCT REPORTED	CARROLL 1-A	ROGGERS 2-B	PRINGLE 3-C	JACOB- LCCI 4-C	MC NICHOLS 5-	PNDUS 6-	SENA- FINI 7-	ARM- STRONG 8-	REDFORD 9-	WEITZGLR 10-C
201	1	246	256	266	241	221	255	237	267	254	247
202	1	345	341	348	308	389	354	341	329	346	302
203	1	273	274	297	249	256	269	250	256	261	261
204	1	265	195	199	193	196	203	186	197	195	191
205	1	240	239	220	234	240	220	238	220	234	216
206	1	145	141	138	127	142	130	133	135	130	137
207	1	273	270	266	240	266	269	266	250	257	247
208	1	326	326	327	301	318	326	310	317	325	278
209	1	344	324	335	322	332	330	322	319	323	290
210	1	309	269	285	286	288	306	285	275	271	257
211	1	323	320	316	318	323	323	324	307	306	280
212	1	287	274	277	256	261	272	262	262	265	233
213	1	463	278	266	240	266	283	257	261	279	252
214	1	293	300	304	282	274	291	278	275	290	202
PREVIOUS TOTAL	14	3904	3849	3820	3610	3720	3867	3646	3661	3735	3442

CITY AND COUNTY OF DENVER
ELECTION RETURN

TITLE: GENERAL ELECTION   DATE: NOV. 6.

PRECINCT	TOTAL PRECINCT REPORTED	US SEN	US REP	SUP CT	SUP CT	GOV	LT GOV	ST SEC	ST AUD	ST TREA	ATT GEN
		CANDIDATES — AMENDMENTS OR BOND ISSUE									
		DOMIN- ICK	CHENG- WETH	CARPEN- TER	HALL	LOVE	GILBERT	ANDER- SON	PROCTOR	ENFIELD	DUNBAR
THIS TOTAL		1-A	2-A	3-A	4-A	5-A	6-A	7-A	8-A	9-A	10-A
1	1	156	120	106	131	173	137	143	116	122	146
2	1	144	122	106	124	168	112	143	121	103	104
3	1	40	82	30	32	39	32	36	31	27	42
4	1	72	59	46	56	85	51	63	47	49	61
5	1	60	46	41	44	49	42	54	44	35	62
6	1	48	36	30	37	58	39	39	34	39	40
7	1	49	29	34	40	67	34	46	36	29	48
8	1	106	81	63	83	116	65	98	79	71	121
9	1	65	47	33	41	70	44	57	63	47	78
10	1	114	78	71	77	116	77	69	73	76	106
11	1	48	26	13	17	47	21	31	17	17	47
12	1	100	83	69	85	123	92	90	64	78	116
13	1	102	84	61	84	132	61	93	94	80	103
14	1	129	109	96	110	149	106	131	110	114	140
	14	1241	958	819	959	1448	958	1107	931	863	1294

CITY AND COUNTY OF DENVER
ELECTION RETURN

TITLE: GENERAL ELECTION   DATE: NOV. 6.

PRECINCT	TOTAL PRECINCT REPORTED	US SEN	US REP	SUP CT	SUP CT	GOV	LT GOV	ST SEC	ST AUD	ST TREA	ATT GEN
		CANDIDATES — AMENDMENTS OR BOND ISSUE									
		DOMIN- ICK	CHENG- WETH	CARPEN- TER	HALL	LOVE	GILBERT	ANDER- SON	PROCTOR	ENFIELD	DUNBAR
PREVIOUS TOTAL		1-A	2-A	3-A	4-A	5-A	6-A	7-A	8-A	9-A	10-A
301	1	30	20	17	19	31	19	27	17	16	24
302	1	71	60	60	55	119	62	85	54	55	73
303	1	63	33	36	41	84	40	59	31	36	64
304	1	72	54	52	65	92	65	73	65	58	80
305	1	58	36	35	39	71	36	46	35	39	47
306	1	60	49	43	43	86	46	48	48	42	93
307	1	43	34	71	33	40	29	36	27	28	30
308	1	100	51	52	51	83	58	56	49	46	61
309	1	32	19	24	19	36	23	21	22	31	37
310	1	72	53	50	56	81	39	49	46	56	56
311	1	25	18	16	19	39	19	24	21	19	27
312	1	66	51	46	44	77	46	49	42	39	73
	12	752	488	447	484	841	482	563	457	450	628

Appendix D-2,3

CITY AND COUNTY OF DENVER

ELECTION RETURN

TITLE: GENERAL ELECTION

DATE: NOV. 5, 196_

PRECINCT	TOTAL PRECINCT REPORTED	US SEN CARROLL 1-B	US REP ROGERS 2-B	SUP CT PRINGLE 3-B	DIST CT JACOBUCCI 4-B	GOVR MC NICHOLS 5-B	LT GOV ENOWS 6-B	ST SEC SERAFINI 7-B	ST AUD ARMSTRONG 8-B	ST TREA REDFEO 9-B	ATT GEN METZGER 10-B
PREVIOUS TOTAL											
301	1	147	130	138	131	147	142	110	142	142	135
302	1	354	323	320	316	312	326	311	313	322	708
303	1	414	415	300	309	304	420	278	418	400	201
304	1	311	281	275	260	283	291	275	282	264	270
305	1	197	203	192	188	184	204	178	193	197	168
306	1	200	200	202	233	250	244	234	236	232	237
307	1	128	121	124	102	130	128	166	114	116	106
308	1	143	149	121	111	120	132	118	120	132	120
309	1	78	73	69	69	77	65	70	74	74	67
310	1	154	165	131	142	154	105	134	146	143	146
311	1	121	103	168	94	111	116	68	103	104	161
312	1	260	247	254	233	245	297	239	247	240	422
TOTAL	12	2553	2459	2402	2233	2392	2495	2273	2391	2406	2291

CITY AND COUNTY OF DENVER
ELECTION RETURN

TITLE: GENERAL ELECTION

DATE: NOV. 6, 196_

PRECINCT	US SEN COMLIN-ICK 1-A	US REP CHENO-WETH 2-A	SUP CT CARPEN-TER 3-A	SUP CT HALL 4-A	GOVR LOVE 5-A	LT GOV GILBERT 6-A	1ST SEC ANDEN-SON 7-A	SY AUD PROCTER 8-A	ST TREA ENFIELD 9-A	ATT GEN DUNBAR 10-A
701	204	160	129	102	221	173	117	103	180	226
702	149	113	104	137	169	127	142	119	114	146
703	65	56	46	59	84	59	48	56	66	72
704	191	174	155	186	204	173	192	180	160	208
705	66	52	34	85	66	58	56	50	62	77
706	150	130	98	122	151	140	135	132	118	104
707	78	78	81	81	97	98	98	86	82	122
708	95	96	72	101	180	90	100	91	93	116
709	71	60	37	90	90	65	55	57	55	65
710	123	100	68	102	137	89	123	109	88	129
711	97	72	54	66	109	71	69	68	66	98
712	40	40	36	44	58	36	38	35	34	45
PREVIOUS TOTAL	1339	1234	660	1176	1503	1124	1326	1187	1109	1687

CANDIDATES — AMENDMENTS OR BOND ISSUE

TOTAL PRECINCT REPORTED: 12

APPENDIX D-5

CITY AND COUNTY OF DENVER
ELECTION RETURN

TITLE: GENERAL ELECTION

DATE: NOV. 6, 196_

SEC

		US SEN	US REP	SUP CT	SUP CT	GOVR	LT GOV	ST SEC	ST SEC	ST ATT GEN	ST ATT GEN
PRECINCT	TOTAL PRECINCT REPORTED		CANDIDATES — AMENDMENTS OR BOND ISSUE								
		CARROLL	ROGERS	PRINGLE	JACOB-UCCI	MC NICHOLS	ANGUS	SEPA-RATE FIN	ANN-STRONG	REDFORD	METZGER
PREVIOUS TOTAL		1-8	2-8	3-8	4-8	5-8	6-8	7-8	8-8	9-8	10-8
701	1	247	260	279	235	224	260	223	233	239	205
702	1	213	221	272	161	192	217	188	205	209	189
703	1	246	243	236	210	231	241	213	226	210	223
704	1	215	229	234	180	202	231	199	146	221	164
705	1	289	261	298	206	284	276	227	233	230	220
706	1	226	228	246	213	221	237	207	217	225	193
707	1	272	246	301	206	254	285	208	222	227	206
708	1	281	248	293	224	258	267	229	248	247	233
709	1	277	282	310	234	256	263	281	250	245	232
710	1	310	360	336	259	297	321	259	272	264	265
711	1	339	332	347	282	329	336	291	206	300	246
712	1	191	175	183	156	172	183	158	160	167	161
	12	3142	3023	3587	2394	2937	3099	2623	2773	2829	2597

Appendix D-6

CITY AND COUNTY OF DENVER
ELECTION RETURN

TITLE GENERAL ELECTION

DATE NOV. 6, 1962

CANDIDATES — AMENDMENTS OR BOND ISSUE

PRECINCT	TOTAL PRECINCT REPORTED	ROBIN-SON	CHENO-WETH	CARPEN-TER YES	HALL	LOWE	GILBERT	ANDER-SON	PROCTOR	ENFIELD	DUNBAR
901	1	128	111	106	120	113	125	135	120	112	153
902	1	236	215	158	203	209	187	230	203	186	201
903	1	128	107	91	131	167	113	142	120	103	147
904	1	144	116	109	141	161	125	140	131	120	175
905	1	126	94	79	111	154	112	126	95	94	134
906	1	112	84	80	101	130	94	123	82	90	134
907	1	212	175	155	192	239	191	211	169	186	234
908	1	132	113	107	126	158	187	100	123	118	142
909	1	95	78	72	84	120	60	67	79	60	94
910	1	154	123	107	139	166	122	148	113	112	161
911	1	171	160	132	175	214	166	160	157	146	193
PREVIOUS TOTAL	11	1648	1370	1187	1527	1223	1480	1672	1488	1343	1830

Appendix D-7

CITY AND COUNTY OF DENVER

ELECTION RETURN

TITLE: GENERAL ELECTION

DATE: NOV. 6, 196_

CANDIDATES — AMENDMENTS OR BOND ISSUE

PRECINCT	TOTAL PRECINCT REPORTED	CARROLL	ROGERS	PRINGLE	JACOB-UCCI	NICHOLS	KNOUS	SERA-FINE	ARN-STRONG	REDFORD	METZGER
PREVIOUS TOTAL											
901	2	247	264	290	214	235	253	227	238	253	256
902	1	342	336	371	314	302	359	306	324	347	174
903	1	267	279	279	231	334	270	230	258	276	230
904	1	144	219	219	172	163	211	164	196	201	161
905	1	263	280	261	244	251	278	253	283	287	256
906	1	183	202	199	168	179	136	160	161	187	160
907	1	300	321	329	274	280	307	274	290	290	207
908	1	233	243	234	200	265	226	193	217	231	193
909	1	174	161	160	138	145	179	166	175	174	100
910	1	273	284	286	244	258	277	240	212	276	246
911	3	244	211	248	203	214	342	216	241	248	312
	11	2752	2682	2904	2414	2462	2798	2455	2570	2776	2377

CITY AND COUNTY OF DENVER

ELECTION RETURN

TITLE: GENERAL ELECTION

DATE: NOV. 6, 1962

SECTI...

PRECINCT	TOTAL PRECINCT REPORTED	1-A	2-A	3-A	4-A	5-A	6-A	7-A	8-A	9-A	10-A
1001	1	39	30	30	32	99	32	38	30	30	36
1002	2	74	62	61	67	95	59	58	62	53	62
1003	3	99	86	76	89	110	82	89	82	71	106
1004	4	60	49	47	50	93	53	55	49	66	60
1005	5	38	49	47	36	41	39	73	24	32	58
1006	6	63	51	51	40	86	50	51	46	44	55
1007	7	61	65	55	59	70	56	54	74	63	73
1008	8	83	71	58	72	77	63	70	74	70	94
1009	9	64	60	68	70	117	86	68	82	70	69
1010	10	60	67	49	53	96	70	57	55	37	61
1011	11	60	68	40	71	80	69	70	67	62	70
PREVIOUS TOTAL	11	744	692	676	643	935	684	674	683	558	793

179

CITY AND COUNTY OF DENVER

ELECTION RETURN

TITLE GENERAL ELECTION

DATE NOV. 6, 196_

CANDIDATES — AMENDMENTS OR BOND ISSUE

Appendix D-10

CITY AND COUNTY OF DENVER

ELECTION RETURN

TITLE: GENERAL ELECTION

DATE NOV. 6, 19__

Appendix D-11

CITY AND COUNTY OF DENVER
ELECTION RETURN

TITLE: GENERAL ELECTION

DATE: NOV. 6, 196?

SECTI

CANDIDATES — AMENDMENTS OR BOND ISSUE

PRECINCT	TOTAL PRECINCT REPORTED	CARROLL	ROGERS	PRINGLE	JACO-UCCI	MC NICHOLS	KNOWN	SEA-FINE	ARM-STRONG	BEDFORD	METZGER
1101	1	178	188	204	169	162	190	170	180	192	157
1102	1	169	171	167	154	164	170	156	163	166	152
1103	1	190	203	190	186	180	190	171	189	200	161
1104	1	200	206	208	166	197	215	165	174	267	176
1105	1	145	139	135	120	136	139	117	180	130	115
1106	1	139	146	146	121	128	148	124	143	147	124
1107	1	284	276	270	219	240		426	243	259	274
1108	1	227	235	227	209	234	234	210	246	233	202
1109	1	149	154	155	141	129	158	144	147	150	141
1110	1	267	301	330	247	276	309	281	261	206	231
1111	1	143	151	152	124	140	163	131	130	148	125
1112	1	266	303	289	259	253	301	253	282	296	231
1113	1	99	108	101	83	89	103	65	74	102	78
PREVIOUS TOTAL	13	2515	2576	2588	2192	2360	2563	2217	2372	2628	2137

Appendix D-12

CITY AND COUNTY OF DENVER
ELECTION RETURN

TITLE: GENERAL ELECTION

DATE: NOV. 6, 19__

CANDIDATES — AMENDMENTS OR BOND ISSUE

Appendix D-13

CITY AND COUNTY OF DENVER
ELECTION RETURN

TITLE: GENERAL ELECTION

DATE: NOV. 6, 196_

PRECINCT	TOTAL PRECINCT REPORTED	US SEN CARROLL 1-B	US REP ROGERS 2-B	SUP CT PRINGLE 3-B	SUP CT JACOBUCCI 4-B	SUP CT MC NICHOLS 5-B	GO B XANGUS 6-B	LT GOV SCRAFINI 7-B	ST SEN ARMSTRONG 8-B	ST SEC BEDFORD 9-B	ST AUD METZGER 10-B
1201	1	366	371	368	326	329	366	320	339	391	307
1202	1	271	240	261	232	234	224	236	250	256	231
1203	1	263	258	310	257	263	305	263	276	293	263
1204	1	209	258	232	204	221	274	212	252	250	226
1205	1	201	208	210	190	184	206	187	194	210	180
1206	1	227	240	229	196	193	223	206	213	218	202
1207	1	213	228	228	213	203	228	201	218	230	201
1208	1	212	210	228	191	194	214	189	205	212	166
1209	1	255	245	252	226	226	263	243	205	258	243
1210	1	172	160	168	142	199	176	160	164	167	150
1211	1	198	205	209	174	181	205	173	183	200	179
PREVIOUS TOTAL	11	2657	2660	2731	2344	2387	2740	2380	2549	2650	2354

CANDIDATES — AMENDMENTS OR BOND ISSUE

Appendix D-14

CITY AND COUNTY OF DENVER
ELECTION RETURN

TITLE GENERAL ELECTION

DATE NOV. 6, 19

Appendix D-15

CITY AND COUNTY OF DENVER

ELECTION RETURN

TITLE: GENERAL ELECTION

DATE: NOV. 5, 196[]

CANDIDATES — AMENDMENTS OR BOND ISSUE

Appendix D-16

CITY AND COUNTY OF DENVER
ELECTION RETURN

TITLE: GENERAL ELECTION

DATE: NOV. 6, 195?

SECTI...

PRECINCT	TOTAL PRECINCT REPORTED	US SEN CORNISH-ICK 1-A	SUP CT CHENO-WITH 2-A	SUP CT CARPEN-TER 1-A	GOVR HALL 4-A	AMENDMENTS — LOVE 5-A	GILBERT 6-A	ANDER-SON 7-A	BOND ISSUE PROCTOR 8-A	BANFIELD 9-A	ATT GEN DUNBAR 10-A
1801	1	42	37	34	30	57	36	43	35	29	49
1802	1	33	26	23	23	40	28	45	28	26	28
1803	1	47	36	29	35	47	29	34	38	30	35
1804	1	39	32	31	31	40	33	40	26	30	49
1805	1	37	29	37	34	43	28	31	26	29	37
1806	1	62	48	53	45	62	56	63	57	49	51
1807	1	52	41	28	42	51	40	43	37	39	54
1808	1	58	42	42	42	58	40	49	47	40	54
1809	1	20	16	10	18	20	17	24	18	20	43
1810	1	42	39	31	34	45	37	35	36	33	34
1811	1	27	23	17	18	29	23	22	16	16	34
1812	1	28	30	26	34	26	25	34	34	25	24
PREVIOUS TOTAL	12	486	398	449	362	475	396	436	393	368	497

Appendix D-17

CITY AND COUNTY OF DENVER

ELECTION RETURN

TITLE: GENERAL ELECTION

DATE: NOV. 6, 19..

	US SEN	US REP	SUP CT	SUP CT	GOV	LT GOV	ST SEC	ST AUD	ST TREA	ATT GEN
			CANDIDATES — AMENDMENTS OR BOND ISSUE							
PRECINCT (TOTAL PRECINCT REPORTED)	CARROLL	ROGERS PRINGLE	PRINGLE	JACOB-UCCI	NICHOLS	KRAOUS	STRA-FINI	ARM-STRONG	PEDFORD	METZGER
	1-8	2-8	3-8	4-8	5-8	6-8	7-8	8-8	9-8	10-8
PREVIOUS TOTAL										
1601 1	194	188	180	173	183	193	176	182	183	171
1602 4	141	123	117	112	129	130	119	119	123	126
1603 1	219	224	214	193	198	225	149	204	205	196
1604 1	227	159	166	164	216	204	174	143	191	178
1605 1	225	262	196	187	204	205	194	155	199	169
1606 1	310	300	279	225	291	287	249	269	271	252
1607 1	207	181	166	148	201	183	148	163	174	160
1608 1	145	144	123	117	142	142	119	125	130	117
1609 1	161	147	145	123	149	154	124	129	134	130
1610 1	132	116	113	102	127	110	106	108	105	97
1611 1	166	141	124	102	156	140	112	119	122	111
1612 1	149	121	114	107	135	130	113	114	114	115
12	2278	2062	1906	1781	2131	2113	1832	1910	1949	1892

Appendix D-18

APPENDIX E

SCHEDULE A FOR RESEARCH SURVEY PANEL

1a. Where were you born? _____ _____
                              Town   State
    Sex: M___ F___

1b. How long have you been in Denver?
    1-5 years___   More than 5 years___   More than 10 years___

1c. How old are you?
    21-30___   31-40___   41-50___   Over 50___

1d. How much education? None___   Grade school only___
    High school___   High school graduate___   Some college___
    College graduate___

2a. What is your occupation?_____
    Marital status: Married___   Single___   Divorced___

2b. How much yearly income in family? Less than $3,000___
    $3,000-$5,000___ $5,100-$7,000___ $7,100-$9,000___
    Over $9,000___

2c. Do you belong to a labor union? Yes___   No___
    How long? Less than 1 year___   1-3 years___   Over 3 years___
    Over 5 years___

3a. Are you a member of a church? Yes___   No___

3b. How often during a year do you attend services?
    A few times___   Often___   Never___   Every Sunday___

3c. How active are you in church organizations?
    Not active___   Somewhat active___   Very active___

3d. How important is a church's position on political candidates and
    political issues? No importance___   Some importance___
    Very important___   Can't say___

3e. How proper do you think it is for priests and ministers to speak in
    behalf of or against some political candidate? Not proper___
    Sometimes proper___   Always proper___   Don't know___

4a. For whom did you vote in the last election? McNichols___   Love___
    Why? Best man___   Best for our people___   Democrat___
    Republican___

4b. How important is it to stick to one's own political party?
Not important___   Not very important___   Quite important___
Very important___

4c. Did you ever vote for someone not of your party?
Never___   2 or 3 times___   Quite a few times___   Often___

5a. Is Spanish spoken in your home?
Never___   Sometimes___   Nearly all the time___   All the time___

5b. Do you want your children to learn and speak Spanish?
Yes___   No___
How important is it?   Not important___   Some importance___
Quite important___   Most important___

5c. Are any members of your family married to Anglos?
Yes___   No___   How many?___
Would you want your son or daughter to marry an Anglo?
Mildly disapprove___   Highly disapprove___   Approve___
Highly approve___

5d. When you go, do you go to a "Spanish" church?
Sometimes___   Never___   Often___   Quite often___

5e. How important is it to be proud of being Spanish?
Not important___   Little important___   Quite important___
Very important___

5f. How strongly do you feel one should forget about being Spanish?
Not very strongly___   Quite strongly___   Very strongly___
Do not feel one should forget___

5g. Do you belong to any "Spanish" organizations or groups?
One___   Two___   Several___   None___

5h. Do you prefer your "own people" as friends and associates?
Sometimes___   Quite often___   Always___   Never___

5i. How about your friends--are they
Mostly Spanish___   Mostly Anglo___   About even___

6a. How much interested are you in the coming election for Mayor?
Not interested___   Little interested___   Quite interested___

6b. Can you name the persons running for mayor in this coming election?
Named all 5___   Named 3 principle ones___   Named 2___
Named 1___   None___

6c. What are your plans as far as voting in the coming city election?
     Do not plan to vote___ May vote___ Definitely will vote___
     Don't know___

6d. If the election were held today, for whom would you vote?
     Batterton___ Currigan___ Grant___ Don't know___

7a. How often do you read newspapers?
     Daily___ Sometimes___ Quite often___ Never___

7b. How often do you listen to the Denver Spanish radio station?
     Daily___ Sometimes___ Quite often___ Never___

7c. How often do you watch the television program "Festival Espanol"?
     Every Sunday___ Once in a while___ Never___

7d. How often do you read a church or religious newspaper or magazine?
     Often___ Sometimes___ Never___

7e. How often do you read a labor newspaper or magazine?
     Often___ Sometimes___ Never___

Name of interviewer_____

Date 1st interview_____
Date 2nd interview_____
Date 3rd interview_____

SCHEDULE B
SECOND PRE-ELECTION INTERVIEW

1. How much interest do you now have in the mayoralty election?
   None at all___ A little interest___ Much interest___
   (If respondent has changed in degree of interest since first inter-
   view, get detailed information on reasons for change).

2. During the past two weeks can you recall reading anything in the
   newspapers about the election or the candidates?
   Yes, read something___ Saw but did not read___
   Did not see or read___

3. During the past two weeks can you remember hearing anything on the
   Spanish radio station about the election or the candidates?
   Yes, heard___ Heard but did not listen___ Did not hear___

4. During the past two weeks can you recall seeing and hearing anything
   on "Festival Espanol" about the election or the candidates?
   Yes, heard & saw___ Saw, but paid no attention___ Did not see___

5. During the past two weeks did you see or read anything about the
   election or the candidates in the Spanish newspaper, "El Tiempo"?
   Saw and read___ Saw but did not read___ Did not see or read___

6. During the past two weeks can you recall discussing the election or
   the candidates or hearing talk about them?
   Yes, discussed___ Yes, heard talk___ Did not hear or discuss___
   (If yes above, what was the occasion? With family, friends, at
   work? What was discussed?)

7. Regardless of how you hope the city election will come out, who do
   you really expect will win? Batterton___ Currigan___ Grant___
   No one, must be a run-off___
   Who do you think will win in the run-off? Batterton___
   Currigan___ Grant___
   On what do you base this opinion? Newspaper reports & polls___
   Opinions of friends___ Just talk___ Conducting best campaign___

8. How strongly do you feel about going to the polls for the city
   election? Sure to vote___ May vote___ Not likely to vote___

9. If the election were held today, for whom would you vote?
   Batterton___ Currigan___ Grant___ Other___ Don't know___
   (If there has been a change, get complete information, put under
   comments).

10. If a choice is indicated in #9, what was the most important reason for your choice of candidate? Best man___ Best for our people___ Best for city problems___ Belongs to my party___

11. If a choice is made in #9, which of the following sources of information or impressions caused you to form your judgement on how to vote? (Rate 1, 2, or 3): Talk with friends___ Knowledge he belonged to my party___ Newspaper articles or editorials___ Watching candidate on TV___ Precinct workers___ Talk with priest___ Labor leader___

12. The following are some of the arguments you hear in this election. For each will you tell me:

	Mildly Agree	Strongly Agree	Mildly Disagree	Strongly Disagree
a. It is time for a change.	___	___	___	___
b. Batterton has done nothing.	___	___	___	___
c. Batterton responsible for "police mess."	___	___	___	___
d. Batterton responsible for "police brutality."	___	___	___	___
e. Currigan "true friend of Hispanos."	___	___	___	___
f. Currigan "tool of 17th Street.	___	___	___	___
g. Grant has long been a true friend of Hispanos	___	___	___	___
h. Grant a rich man, tool of 17th Street	___	___	___	___
i. Grant best qualified, does not need job to get rich.	___	___	___	___
j. The present mayor is mostly responsible for "poor condition" of Denver General Hospital	___	___	___	___

13. For each of the candidates, indicate what best describes the various candidates:
Batterton: Good personality___ Outstanding personality___ Fair personality___ Poor personality___
Currigan: Good personality___ Outstanding personality___ Fair personality___ Poor personality___
Grant: Good personality___ Outstanding personality___ Fair personality___ Poor personality___

14. Which would be best for the "Spanish people"?
Batterton___ Currigan___ Grant___
Why?

15. Whom do you consider the leaders in the Spanish community?

_____ ___
Names   None

16. Do you know or have you heard about the following leaders or so-called leaders among the Spanish people? Dave Martinez___
"Corky" Gonzales___ Bernie Valdez___ James Fresquez___
"Paco" Sanchez___ Tim Duran___ Bert Gallegos___ Dan Valdes___

17. Have you done anything to help get your candidate elected?
Yes___ No___ Don't know___

18. Do you ever read the editorials in the newspapers?
Never___ Quite often___ Frequently___ Almost always___
What newspapers?_____

19. Have you listened to any political speeches or to candidates for mayor on television or radio?
Never___ Frequently___ A few times___ Don't know___

20. Have you read any of the editorials or articles on the election in the Spanish newspaper "El Tiempo"?
Never___ A few times___ Frequently___ Don't know___

SCHEDULE C
POST-ELECTION INTERVIEW

1. Did you vote in the May 21, 1963 mayoralty election? Yes___   No___

2. If you did not vote, why not? Too busy___   Not interested___
   Not important enough___   Did not like candidates___
   Unable to get to polls___

3. If you did vote, what was the most important reason for voting?
   Urging of friends___   Urging of husband or wife___
   A citizen's duty___   Great interest in election___
   Important for our people to vote___   Urging of party workers___

4. For whom did you finally vote?
   Currigan___   Batterton___   Grant___   Other___

5. What was the main reason for voting for this candidate? Party___
   Best for Hispano people___   Best man___   Other___(Specify)

6. What affect did seeing and hearing the candidates have in your final
   decision to vote for a certain candidate? None___   A little___
   Quite a bit___   A great deal___

7. What affect did reading about the candidates have on your decision?
   None___   A little___   Quite a bit___   A great deal___

8. What affect did the advice of friends and relatives have on your
   decision? None___   A little___   Quite a bit___   A great deal___

9. What affect did the possibility that one candidate was better for
   "our people" have on your decision?
   None___   A little___   Quite a bit___   A great deal___

10. What affect did reading articles in "El Tiempo" have on your
    decision? None___   A little___   Quite a bit___   A great deal___

Appendix F

Racial Composition and Persons
of Spanish Surname, By Census Tract
Denver Metropolitan Area, 1960

Tract No.	Total Population	Persons of Spanish Surname		Non-White	
		Native-born	Foreign Born	Negro	Other
1-A	3,520	85	4	4	15
1-B	4,665	77	4	7	24
2-A	4,568	189		2	35
2-B	5,364	988	16	133	61
3-A	6,695	373	16	1	24
3-B	11,392	276	12	3	34
4-A	4,019	332	28	1	46
4-B	7,892	1,189	45	22	99
5	8,401	376	40	20	62
6	3,584	657	12	6	31
7	8,935	1,579	26	133	94
8	4,138	2,284	60	365	72
9-A	6,613	863	12	57	44
9-B	5,887	506	4	36	39
9-C	5,296	388	4	21	10
10	4,388	472	8	40	24
11-A	3,371	1,146	52	81	69
11-B	4,165	1,149	71	3	76
12	1,519	832	31	19	46
13	9,400	293	9	5	24
14-A	9,797	484	4	13	32
14-B	3,574	239	4	32	3
15	5,294	1,445	27	559	302
16	1,876	904	127	214	152
17-A	1,359	63	9	30	100
17-B	4,680	312	23	104	163
18	3,717	1,418	24	58	32
19	5,552	2,993	58	484	89
20	2,649	410	29	2	39
21	8,075	1,680	16	5	32
22	5,821	2,808	199	1,589	249
23	8,731	396	3	7,438	101
24-A	6,201	2,410	46	2,600	345
24-B	3,168	194		2,614	29
25	2,023	591	21	108	71
26-A	4,814	125		30	43
26-B	3,301	154	21	11	66
27-A	6,107	122		1	61
27-B	4,769	57	11	4	41
27-C	5,995	133	4	1	65

Appendix F

Racial Composition and Persons
of Spanish Surname, By Census Tract
Denver Metropolitan Area, 1960

196

Tract No.	Total Population	Persons of Spanish Surname		Non-White	
		Native-born	Foreign Born	Negro	Other
28-A	3,434	67	28	4	18
28-B	7,988	153	4	2	19
29	9,758	283	8	1	26
30-A	8,070	104		1	23
30-B	3,576	72		15	4
30-C	10,203	100	16	38	53
31-A	3,009	96		466	2,465
31-B	5,228	274	8	532	83
32-A	7,739	172	13	19	104
32-B	3,996	46		36	9
33	4,112	86	4	1	9
34	8,532	58		1	12
35-A	4,357	700	51	44	26
35-B	2,315	543	27	179	22
36-A	7,259	2,161	107	2,573	114
36-B	5,172	489	7	2,630	298
36-C	4,785	135	13	3,512	256
37-A	2,898	62	8	1	29
37-B	8,641	167	24	6	93
38	5,300	68	4	129	34
39-A	3,855	64		16	9
39-B	5,616	59	8	4	5
40-A	6,478	104	4	4	20
40-B	3,893			3	3
40-C	7,057	61		3	2
40-D	1,215		3		6
41-A	9,282	366		361	79
41-B	7,044	89		314	71
41-C	5,930	88		18	24
42-A	6,203	20		5	22
42-B	5,264	50	8	3	9
43-A	9,289	168	13	25	50
43-B	5,270	37		24	25
43-C	7,396	181	8	18	24
43-D	3,541	25	3	9	5
44-A	7,846	205	8	4	72
44-B	7,781	111		4	334
45-A	6,839	759	9	1	28
45-B	7,229	1,649	56	117	79
46-A	7,429	127			10

Racial Composition and Persons
of Spanish Surname, By Census Tract
Denver Metropolitan Area, 1960   197

Tract No.	Total Population	Persons of Spanish Surname		Non-White	
		Native-born	Foreign Born	Negro	Other
46-B	4,887	40		1	14
46-C	7,521	114		1	25
47	5,955	94		1	19
48	9,111	235	15	3	49
49	1,679	11	12	10	1
50	2,987	71		2	9
51	8,264	87		1	26
52	3,192				3
53	2,032				5
54	4,709	577	9	20	35
55	7,474	323	8	36	11
56	11,539	208	20	16	20
57	4,275	208		6	35
58	3,770	89		2	22
59	6,156	139	4	1	27
60	4,182	106		66	28
61	3,397	40		1	12
62	4,337	48	16	4	11
63	4,079	120			11
64	3,128	27	4	1	29
65	5,888	240			19
66	8,377	36		2	12
67	2,712	39		26	6
68	459	10		49	5
69	2,649			8	6
70	2,780	94		46	3
71	1,827		4	12	7
72	5,553	60			13
73	6,197	123	3	8	43
74	6,161	97		6	25
75	3,672	80		1	7
76	3,679	109	8	3	19
77	1,753	37			11
78	4,113	103	15	2	53
79	4,505	91	8	1	17
80	6,115	88		3	35
81	2,095	34	3	195	48
82	2,644	82		3	35
83	3,036	31	8	7	20
84	1,862	14		1	

Racial Composition and Persons
of Spanish Surname, By Census Tract
Denver Metropolitan Area, 1960   198

Tract No.	Total Population	Persons of Spanish Surname		Non-White	
		Native-Born	Foreign Born	Negro	Other
85	5,981	512	35	62	300
86	6,843	1,562	24	7	70
87	11,740	1,069	7	72	95
88	9,606	820	12	12	91
89	6,662	818	34	180	128
90	3,846	211	4	7	65
91	6,566	670	27	3	25
92	5,052	431	21	18	27
93	10,834	521	20	13	107
94	3,972	33			29
95	10,591	662		10	115
96	10,215	460	16	26	73
97	4,018	96		11	29
98	8,885	151	13	12	19
99	3,152	81	16		11
100	3,966	141	5	16	41
101	2,604	4			3
102	5,339	40		1	17
103	12,275	72		1	23
104	10,065	250		8	26
105	6,813	149		11	8
106	8,571	152	4	1	11
107	8,345	184	4	2	14
108	3,938	91	4		
109	3,650	171		2	8
110	5,266	97			14
111	4,872	101		1	14
112	4,684	93		1	
113	4,222	130		17	19
114	3,884	126	4	5	26
115	5,075	73		2	11
116	4,932	71			10
117	3,257	31		4	9
118	7,330	180		12	20
119	267	14		3	4
120	6,893	107		34	62

Source: U.S. Census of Population, 1960
Issued by Denver Planning Office, November 21, 1961

DISTRICT 2

REGISTRATION TOTALS------------OCTOBER 22, 1962

PRECINCT	Rep.	Dem.	Ind.	Total
201	82	283	200	565
202	81	396	279	756
203	44	338	145	527
204	39	221	122	382
205	51	381	121	553
206	28	273	56	357
207	35	399	102	536
208	61	382	215	658
209	36	403	144	583
210	46	363	191	600
211	20	423	125	568
212	78	349	154	581
213	102	427	214	743
214	98	432	161	691
	801	5,070	2,229	8,100

VOTE TOTALS--------------------NOVEMBER 6, 1962

PCT.	Love	McN.	Total	Dom.	Carr.	Total	Chen.	Rog.
201	179	221	400	156	246	402	120	258
202	162	329	491	144	348	492	122	341
203	59	256	315	40	273	313	28	274
204	85	196	281	75	205	280	59	195
205	69	240	309	60	249	309	46	239
206	58	142	200	48	145	193	36	141
207	67	266	333	49	273	322	39	270
208	116	318	434	106	326	432	81	326
209	75	332	407	65	344	409	47	334
210	118	305	423	114	309	423	78	299
211	57	323	380	48	323	371	26	320
212	123	261	384	105	287	392	83	274
213	132	266	398	102	283	385	84	278
214	148	274	422	129	293	422	109	300
	1,448	3,729	5,177	1,241	3,904	5,145	958	3,849

200

DISTRICT 3

REGISTRATION TOTALS----------------------------October 22, 1962

PRECINCT	REP.	DEM.	IND.	TOTAL
301	35	231	33	289
302	48	626	102	776
303	37	620	74	731
304	44	438	72	554
305	65	438	113	616
306	36	547	102	685
307	37	259	62	358
308	39	305	86	430
309	42	166	81	289
310	41	300	89	430
311	22	202	51	275
312	35	397	73	505
TOTAL	471	4,529	938	5,938

VOTE TOTALS----------------------------------November 6, 1962

Pct.	Love	McN.	Total	Dom.	Carr.	Total	Chen.	Rog.
301	31	142	173	30	147	177	26	139
302	119	312	431	71	354	425	60	323
303	84	384	468	63	414	477	33	415
304	92	283	375	72	311	383	54	291
305	71	184	255	58	197	255	36	203
306	88	250	338	60	286	346	49	260
307	40	130	170	43	128	171	36	121
308	83	120	203	160	143	303	51	129
309	36	77	113	32	78	110	19	73
310	81	154	235	72	154	226	53	155
311	39	111	150	25	121	146	18	103
312	77	245	322	66	260	326	51	247
	841	2,392	3,233	752	2,593	3,345	486	2,459

DISTRICT 7

Precinct	Repb.	Dem.	Ind.	Total
701	134	299	222	655
702	98	286	179	563
703	48	332	142	522
704	126	252	229	607
705	30	448	127	605
706	95	314	246	655
707	59	318	158	535
708	79	303	219	601
709	32	335	159	526
710	75	464	165	704
711	61	659	235	955
712	46	407	119	572
TOTAL	883	4,417	2,200	7,500

VOTE TOTALS

Pct.	Love	McN.	Total	Dom.	Carr.	Total	Chen.	Rog.
701	221	224	445	204	247	451	168	260
702	159	192	351	149	213	362	113	221
703	84	231	315	66	246	312	56	243
704	204	202	406	191	215	406	174	229
705	68	284	352	66	289	355	52	261
706	151	221	372	150	226	376	130	228
707	97	254	351	78	272	350	76	246
708	120	258	378	95	281	376	96	258
709	95	259	354	71	277	348	50	282
710	137	297	434	123	316	439	106	288
711	109	333	443	97	339	436	73	332
712	58	172	230	49	191	240	40	175
	1,503	2,927	4,430	1,339	3,112	4,451	1,134	3,023

DISTRICT 9

REGISTRATION TOTALS---------------------October 22, 1962

Precinct	Repb.	Dem.	Ind.	Total
901	106	288	188	582
902	144	363	357	864
903	71	314	229	614
904	109	219	224	552
905	81	323	211	615
906	86	264	135	485
907	142	349	257	748
908	89	300	192	581
909	60	200	113	373
910	102	322	241	665
911	130	296	242	668
TOTAL	1,120	3,238	2,389	6,747

VOTE TOTALS--------------------------November 6, 1962

Pct.	Love	McN.	Total	Dom.	Carr.	Total	Chen.	Rog.
901	153	235	388	138	247	385	111	264
902	259	302	561	236	322	558	215	336
903	167	234	401	128	267	395	107	279
904	161	183	344	144	194	338	116	215
905	156	251	407	126	283	409	94	286
906	130	175	305	112	193	305	84	202
907	239	280	519	212	300	512	175	321
908	158	205	363	132	233	365	113	243
909	120	145	265	95	174	269	78	181
910	166	258	424	154	275	429	123	284
911	214	214	428	171	244	415	160	251
	1,923	2,482	4,405	1,648	2,732	4,380	1,376	2,862

DISTRICT 10

REGISTRATION TOTALS---------------------October 22, 1962

PRECINCT	REPB.	DEM.	IND.	TOTAL
1001	28	457	82	567
1002	57	410	96	563
1003	85	328	101	514
1004	56	563	108	727
1005	27	251	93	371
1006	40	449	110	599
1007	44	292	168	504
1008	52	193	154	399
1009	81	355	145	581
1010	41	400	114	555
1011	66	316	102	484
TOTAL	577	4,014	1,273	5,864

VOTE TOTALS

Pct.	Love	McN.	Total	Dom.	Carr.	Total	Chen.	Rog.
1001	59	230	289	39	246	285	38	241
1002	95	238	333	74	255	329	62	241
1003	110	200	310	99	207	306	84	207
1004	93	305	398	69	322	391	59	307
1005	41	150	191	38	151	189	25	151
1006	89	267	356	63	291	354	55	274
1007	70	210	280	61	209	270	55	204
1008	97	158	255	83	167	250	71	163
1009	117	213	330	84	239	323	80	231
1010	98	226	324	66	264	330	57	247
1011	86	215	301	88	213	301	66	211
	955	2,412	3,367	764	2,564	3,328	652	2,477

DISTRICT 11

REGISTRATION TOTALS--------------------October 22, 1962

PRECINCT	REPB.	DEM.	IND.	TOTAL
1101	118	260	233	611
1102	63	308	95	466
1103	84	259	142	485
1104	93	366	142	601
1105	119	206	105	430
1106	98	254	127	479
1107	134	300	284	718
1108	108	323	202	633
1109	49	230	90	369
1110	194	330	304	828
1111	75	264	106	445
1112	110	361	244	715
1113	66	169	95	330
TOTAL	1,311	3,630	2,169	7,110

VOTE TOTALS--

Pct.	Love	McN.	Total	Dom.	Carr.	Total	Chen.	Rog.
1101	169	162	331	154	178	332	132	188
1102	92	166	258	90	169	259	74	171
1103	122	190	312	105	199	304	93	203
1104	137	197	334	133	200	333	115	206
1105	118	138	256	108	145	253	99	139
1106	130	128	258	120	139	259	102	145
1107	223	246	469	186	284	470	168	276
1108	146	224	370	134	227	361	104	235
1109	67	139	206	56	149	205	51	154
1110	276	276	552	249	297	546	227	301
1111	95	146	241	94	143	237	72	151
1112	183	259	442	153	286	439	128	303
1113	71	89	160	58	99	157	50	106
	1,829	2,360	4,189	1,640	2,515	4,155	1,415	2,578

DISTRICT 12

REGISTRATION TOTALS----------------------October 22, 1962

PRECINCT	REPB.	DEM.	IND.	TOTAL
1201	117	408	282	807
1202	125	430	195	750
1203	111	353	324	788
1204	148	382	262	792
1205	63	293	142	498
1206	95	347	225	667
1207	119	372	170	661
1208	87	280	184	551
1209	65	381	201	647
1210	49	227	144	420
1211	73	326	191	590
TOTAL	1,052	3,799	2,320	7,171

VOTE TOTALS------------------------------November 6, 1962

Pct.	Love	McN.	Total	Dom.	Carr.	Total	Chen.	Rog.
1201	195	329	524	159	366	525	130	371
1202	203	234	437	165	271	436	153	260
1203	192	263	455	171	283	454	151	295
1204	235	221	456	212	259	471	176	258
1205	112	184	296	100	201	301	74	208
1206	161	193	354	126	227	353	119	220
1207	135	203	338	117	213	330	93	228
1208	144	194	338	126	212	338	116	210
1209	118	226	344	81	255	336	77	245
1210	98	159	257	86	172	258	88	160
1211	142	181	323	120	198	318	102	205
	1,735	2,387	4,122	1,463	2,657	4,120	1,279	2,660

DISTRICT 15

PRECINCT	REPB.	DEM.	IND.	TOTAL
1501	16	276	45	337
1502	38	316	75	429
1503	64	372	154	590
1504	80	415	236	731
1505	37	189	83	309
1506	30	460	110	600
1507	26	490	83	599
1508	49	406	135	590
1509	16	304	94	414
1510	30	419	140	589
1511	39	469	170	678
1512	63	366	143	572
1513	40	358	113	511
TOTAL	528	4,840	1,581	6,949

VOTE TOTALS-

Pct.	Love	McN.	Total	Dom.	Carr.	Total	Chen.	Rog.
1501	45	152	197	36	163	199	30	162
1502	78	190	268	64	209	273	56	198
1503	108	249	357	84	279	363	58	282
1504	173	270	443	143	299	442	114	293
1505	57	121	178	45	131	176	35	131
1506	69	195	264	48	221	269	41	209
1507	46	227	273	35	240	275	22	224
1508	75	217	292	52	252	304	41	225
1509	39	201	240	32	211	243	22	212
1510	66	269	335	55	281	336	41	273
1511	76	256	332	60	277	337	44	275
1512	80	249	329	66	259	325	48	243
1513	43	197	240	38	207	245	24	201
	955	2,793	3,748	758	3,029	3,787	576	2,928

DISTRICT 18

REGISTRATION TOTALS----------------------October 22, 1962

PRECINCT	REPB.	DEM.	IND.	TOTAL
1801	56	348	68	472
1802	25	241	64	330
1803	44	417	12^	581
1804	43	394	118	555
1805	46	399	96	541
1806	64	482	156	7^2
1807	64	339	81	484
1808	52	230	97	379
1809	20	279	97	396
1810	49	335	76	460
1811	37	232	95	364
1812	20	309	59	388
TOTAL	520	4,005	1,127	5,652

VOTE TOTALS

Pct.	Love	McN.	Total	Dom.	Carr.	Total	Chen.	Rog.
1801	57	183	240	42	194	236	37	188
1802	40	129	169	33	141	174	28	123
1803	67	198	265	47	219	266	36	224
1804	40	216	256	35	227	262	32	195
1805	47	204	251	37	225	262	29	202
1806	82	291	373	65	310	375	48	300
1807	51	201	252	52	207	259	41	181
1808	56	142	198	58	145	203	42	144
1809	29	149	178	20	161	181	16	147
1810	48	127	175	42	132	174	39	116
1811	29	156	185	27	166	193	22	141
1812	29	135	164	28	149	177	26	121
	575	2,131	2,706	486	2,276	2,762	396	2,082

TEXT OF TALK OVER SPANISH TELEVISION PROGRAM

Buenas noches senoras y senores. Con su permiso voy
hablar en ingles porque no tengo mas de cinco minutos, y la
mayoria de ustedes comprenden bien el ingles.

Those of you who are older than 35 know who Fiorello H.
LaGuardia was. He was the little Italian-Jew in the 1930's
who was only the greatest mayor New York City ever had.

Well, last February, in El Tiempo, we said that Denver
was crying for a LaGuardia. We carried a full page cartoon
on the subject. (Close up of first cartoon for only a few
seconds). La Guardia was vigorous, fearless, dynamic, and
human. When we say that he was human, we don't mean he was
alive, his body warm, his heart beating. The thing that makes
a mayor human is how he lives, how much warmth of the soul he
has, what he feels in his heart, not that his heart is merely
beating.

We want a mayor that is so alive that some things make
him fighting made, I want him to rant and rave about little
kids having to live and grow up in the squalor of Denver's
slums--oh, yes, we have them. I want him to fire the inspector
that reaps his harvest of booze and petty graft, just as quickly
as I want him to throw in jail the cop that is caught red-handed
in the super-market safe. I want a mayor who is indignant, even
fighting mad, about things that are evil in our city.

We said last February that, like LaGuardia, we want to see
in Denver's next mayor, a man who is fearless, dynamic, and vigorous.

Sounds corny, but why shouln't a dynamic and vigorous city have a mayor
to match?

There is a person running for mayor who will give all people in
Denver, including the Hispano American, proper representation in city
government, who will vigorously carry on a fight against all types of
discrimination, who will protect us against police violence and at the
same time fight against crime and the evil elements in both our own
cultural group and in the general population. There is a man running
for mayor of Denver who will do everything he can to make available better homes and better streets and parks for the less economically favored
and will rid Denver of its slums. Yes, we have found a La Guardia for
mayor of Denver. I hope you agree with me and vote for Bill Grant for
mayor this coming Tuesday. (Close-up on second cartoon, hold for few
seconds). This man is a registered Democrat running on a non-partisan
basis. He deserves our support. Let's give him a shove up those stairs
right into the mayor's executive chambers.

I have just read Bill Grant's eight point program, which he calls
a "Design for Destiny." Our destiny, ladies and gentlemen, and that of
our children. The things that we cried out for in our February article
are in the "Design for Destiny." (1) Equal opportunity for all citizens
regardless of race, creed or national origin. This, I believe, because
Bill Grant, like LaGuardia, has practiced what he preaches. (2) A
dynamic plan for economic growth with job security for Denver citizens--
not political jobs, but jobs in new industries, in a healthy, dynamic

economy. With this kind of economy we won't be the last hired or the first fired. (3) A safe, clean city with proper lighting and street care for all parts of the city, not just where the higher income people live. (4) Outstanding health facilities that will replace the unsafe, dingy wards of Denver General Hospital--but leaving it where it now is so that those who need it most can get there easily and cheaply. (5) Improved social and cultural opportunities for all the citizens of Denver. Have you seen the dilapidated, poorly maintained community centers in areas where some of our people live? (6) Metropolitan solidarily which will bring some 20,000 fellow Hispano Americans into the city with us. (7) A non-partisan administration where our people won't have to beg political bosses and ward heelers for jobs and favors due them as citizens, and finally, (8) an international airport to bring us culturally and economically closer to all our cultural brothers throughout Hispano America.

Yes, we have found a LaGuardia for Denver. Let's vote for Bill Grant for mayor this Tuesday. Be sure to vote and to vote for this man.

EL TIEMPO

A COMPENDIUM OF NEWS AND OTHER VITAL INFORMATION RELATING TO THE NATIONS AND PEOPLES OF THE VASTLY IMPORTANT HISPANIC WORLD

VOL 1 — NO. 43

DENVER, COLORADO

Thursday, May 16, 1963

We Must Show Strength By Voting On May 21

Should Not Complain If We Fail To Vote Against Those Responsible For Our Status

"El Tiempo" urges all Americans, especially those with Spanish names, to be sure to vote at the city election this coming Tuesday, May 21. For quite a few years we have heard the crying and complaining of many Hispano Americans because of differential treatment on the part of Denver police, of discrimination in employment, of almost a complete lack of representation on city boards and commissions, of poorly lighted and poorly maintained streets in areas of the city where Hispanos are more or less concentrated and the lack of new industries to stimulate employment which would be most helpful to the increasingly larger number of skilled and semi-skilled workers among our people. We have not been able to do anything about these conditions because we have not been able to use our most powerful weapon—the voting fran-

chise. Here's your golden and only opportunity to correct the abuses against, and the neglect of, Americans with Spanish names in Denver.

The only fear the politicians know and recognize is the vote of those whom they have abused and neglected during their term of office. Americans of Spanish descent and of Mexican descent have been abused and neglected because they have not used their. votes against those who are their enemies. For all you hold dear, vote this Tuesday—show your strength and your convictions.

It has always been the privilege—and the duty—of Americans to throw out or out of office those who have gone against the welfare of all the people of a city, state or nation. Do not overlook this privilege or neglect this duty.

We cannot honestly say vote for

anyone, but vote, because it is most important for whom you vote.

It is your duty to vote against

Cont. page 3

All Hispanos Non-White To Denver Police Dept.

Judging from the 1960 Denver Police Department Annual Report, "Spanish" persons arrested for crimes or on suspicion of committing crimes in Denver are by direct and clear implication members of the colored race.

In reporting on the number of

crimes committed for different categories of crimes, Denver police recognize only five divisions in the Denver population—"white", "negro", "indian", "yellow", and "Spanish".

The statistics presented in the
Cont. page 5

Anti-Discrimination Director Exam A Farce And Travesty Of Justice

Members of Oral Exam Board Were Not Eligible

Leaving aside all other considerations and factors, no one in his right mind can deny the fact that oral examinations are always highly subjective affairs in which the personal likes and dislikes, biases and prejudices of all sorts of those conducting the examina-

tion of director of the Colorado Anti-Discrimination Commission. After all, they are human beings.

But oral "competitive" exams of this sort become a farce and a travesty on good government and justice (as indeed it was in the

---

A LESSON ON HOW TO DIVIDE AND CONQUER MINORITIES IN DENVER

....
NEXT WEEK

EL TIEMPO

DENVER, COLORADO

THURSDAY, APRIL 25, 19

DANIEL T. VALDÉS, MANAGING EDITOR
RUBÉN C. VALDEZ, NEWS EDITOR

ENRIQUE GARCIA, ADVERTISING MANAGE
ARMANDO CAMPERO, ARTIST
HUMBERT NUÑOZ, PHOTOGRAPHER

VOL. 1 — NO. 43

How "Spanish" Are Denver Hispanos?

FIRST COMPLETE SURVEY BEGINS

SOCIO-ECONOMIC CHARACTERISTICS & POLITICAL BEHAVIOR UNDER STUDY

Will Denver Americans with Spanish names vote for another "Spanish-name" political candidate regardless of political party? Will they vote against a candidate for political office whom they feel is "bad" for "the Spanish people" even if it means voting against their own political party? The answers to these and many other questions are being sought in a public opinion survey now being conducted in Denver by a research team headed by Daniel T. Valdes, Editor of "El Tiempo".

What proportion of Denver Hispano workers belong to labor unions? How active are they in church organizations? How many speak and understand Spanish? Do they feel that speaking Spanish is important? What papers do they read? What radio and TV programs do they hear and watch? How do they feel about their sons or daughters marrying Anglo-Americans? These are additional questions that have already been asked in the first phase of the interviewing which was completed this week. Nearly 400 Hispano Americans were interviewed during the first phase of the research.

During the first interview, nearly 400 registered Hispano voters were also asked for whom they would vote for mayor as of the time of the interview. Nearly three-fourths had still not made up their minds. Many did not even know who the candidates are. There know who the candidates are. These same voters will be immediately twice more before the mayoralty election and once immediately after the election in an effort to determine what makes them vote the way they do – the impact of mass media, the importance of friends and relatives and precinct workers in making up their minds, etc.

SANTA FE THEATRE DRAWING WELL

A few months ago, Mr. and Mrs. Rodolfo Nunez, better known proprietors of La Bonita Enterprises, purchased the Santa Fe Theatre with the policy of presenting Mexican and American pictures regularly on the same program.

That movie house had been operated spasmodically for several years and was often closed during long periods, so its revival was not easy. However, the news management has succeeded beyond their expectations and is now drawing substantial clientele.

An amateur night on Monday and movie sweepstakes on Thursday seem to have broken the grand interest in being demonstrated. We wish them well, it is certain that Mexican movies will continue to be available

CODING INSTRUCTIONS

Col.		Scale Item	Code	Description
1	1	1 a	0 1, 2	Colo. N.M. Other
	2	1 b	0 1 2	One to five years More than 5 years More than 10 years
	3	1 c	0 1 2 3	Between 21 & 30 Between 31 & 40 Between 41 & 50 Over 50
	4	1 d	0 1 2 3 4 5	None Grade School only High School High School graduate Some college College graduate
	5	2 b	0 1 2 3 4	Less than $3,000.00 $3,100. - $5,000.00 $5,100. - $7,000.00 $7,100. - $9,000.00 Over $9,000
	6	2 c	0 1	No Member of labor union Yes
	7	3 a	0 1	No Member of church Yes
	8	3 b	0 1 2 3	Never Attends church A few times Often Every Sunday
	9	3 c	0 1 2	Not active in church organizations Somewhat active Very active

Appendix J.

CODING INSTRUCTIONS
(Continued)

Col.	Scale Item	Code	Description
10	3 d	0	No importance to church position on politics
		1	Some importance
		2	Very important
		3	Don't know or wouldn't say
11	3 c	0	Not proper for priests to speak in favor of political candidates
		1	Sometimes proper
		2	Always proper
		3	Don't know

Col.	Scale Item	Code	Description
12	4 a	0	McNichols
		1	Love
13	4 aa	0	Voted for McNichols because of party
		1	Voted for McNichols because best man
		2	Voted for McNichols because "best man for our people"
		3	Voted for Love because of party
		4	Voted for Love because "best man"
		5	Voted for Love because "best for our people"
14	4 b	0	No importance to sticking to one's own party
		1	Not very importatn
		2	Quite important
		3	Very important
15	4 c	0	Often votes for someone not of own party
		1	Quite a few times
		2	Never
16	5 a	0	Spanish never spoken in home
		1	Sometimes
		2	Nearly all the time
		3	All the time
17	5 b	0	Doesn't want children to speak Spanish
		1	Wants children to speak Spanish
18	5 bb	0	No importance to children learning and speaking Spanish
		1	Some importante
		2	Quite important
		3	Most important
19	5 c	0	Members of family married to Anglos
		1	No members married to Anglos
20	5 cc	0	Highly approves marriage of son or daughter to Anglo
		1	Approves
		2	Mildly disapproves
		3	Highly disapproves
21	5 d	0	Never goes to "Spanish" church
		1	Sometimes
		2	Often
		3	Quite often

Col.	Scale Item	Code	Description
22	5 e	0 1 2 3	Not important being "Spanish" Little importance Quite important Very important
23	5 f	0 1 2	Feels strongly one should forget being "Spanish" Not very strongly Feels one should not forget
24	5 h	0 1 2 3	Never prefers "own people" as friends Sometimes Quite often Always
25	5 i	0 1 2	Friends, mostly Anglos Friends, about even Friends, mostly Spanish
26	6 a	0 1 2	Not much interested in election Little Interested Quite interested
27	6 c	0 1 2 3	Does not plan to vote May vote Definitely will vote Don't know
28	6 d	0 1 2 3	For Batterton For Currigan For Grant Don't know
29	7 a	0 1 2 3	Never reads newspapers Sometimes Quite often Daily
30	7 b	0 1 2 3	Never listens to Spanish radio Sometimes Quite often Daily
31	7 c	0 1 2	Never watches Spanish TV Once in a while Every Sunday

Col.	Scale Item	Code	Description
32	7 d	0	Never reads church or religious newspaper or magazine
		1	Sometimes
		2	Often
33	7 e	0	Never reads labor magazines or newspapers
		1	Sometimes
		2	Often
34	2	0	Did not read or see
		1	Saw but did not read
		2	Yes, read
35	3	0	Did not hear on radio
		1	Heard, did not listen
		2	Yes, heard
36	4	0	Did not see on TV
		1	Saw, paid no attention
		2	Heard and saw
37	5	0	Did not see or read
		1	Saw, did not read
		2	read
38	6	0	Did not hear or discuss
		1	Heard talk
		2	Discussed
39	8	0	Not likely to vote
		1	Fairly likely to vote
		2	Sure to vote
41	10	0	Belongs to party
		1	Best man
		2	Best for city
		3	"Best for our people"
42	11	0	Belonged to party
		1	Newspaper articles and editorials
		2	TV programs
		3	Friends and neighbors
		4	Precinct workers
43	14	0	Best for our people / Batterton
		1	Currigan
		2	Grant
		3	Don't know

Col.	Scale item	Code	Description
44	18		Read editorials
		0	Never
		1	Quite often
		2	Frequently
		3	Almost always
45	19		Listened to political material on TV or ratio
		0	Never
		1	A few times
		2	Frequently
		3	Don't know
46	20		Read editorials or articles on election in "El Tiempo"
		0	Never
		1	A few times
		2	Frequently
47	3-1	0	Did not vote
		1	Voted
48	3-4		Voted for
		0	Batterton
		1	Currigan
		2	Grant
49	3-5		Main reason for voting for candidate
		0	Party
		1	Best man
		2	"Best for our people"
		3	"other"
50	3-7		Affect hearing and seeing candidates
		0	None
		1	Little
		2	Quite a bit
		3	A great deal
51	3-9		What effect did friends and relatives have
		0	None
		1	A little
		2	Quite a bit
		3	A great deal
52	3-11		Affect reading articles in El Tiempo
		0	None
		1	A little
		2	Quite a bit
		3	A great deal

Col.	Scale Item	Code	Description
53	5f, 5h, 5d, 5c, 5a, 5b, 5e	xxxx5, 0, 2, 3, 4, 5, 6, 7	Ethnicity
54	7a, 7b, 7c, 7d, 7e, 2-2, 2-3, 2-4, 2-5	0, 1, 2, 3, 4, 5, 6, 7, 8	Exposure
55	3a, 3b, 3c, 3d, 3e	0, 1, 2, 3, 4, 5	Traditionalism
56	As per orientation index 4a, 4b, 4c	0, 1, 2, 3	Party Loyalty
57	B-1	0, 1, 2	Interest in election second interview None Little interest Much interest
58	C-1	0, 1	Did not vote Voted
59	B-8	0, 1, 2	Intention to vote Not likely to vote Failry likely to vote Sure to vote
60	13-9	0, 1, 2, 3	Choice of candidate second interview Batterton Currigan Grant Don't know

Col.	Scale item	Code	Description
61	C-5		Choice of candidate third interview
		0	Batterton
		1	Currigan
		2	Grant
		3	Other
62	C-5		Main reason for voting for candidate
		0	Party
		1	Best man
		2	Best for Hispanos
		3	Ither

THE CHICANO HERITAGE

An Arno Press Collection

Adams, Emma H. **To and Fro in Southern California.** 1887

Anderson, Henry P. **The Bracero Program in California.** 1961

Aviña, Rose Hollenbaugh. **Spanish and Mexican Land Grants in California.** 1976

Barker, Ruth Laughlin. **Caballeros.** 1932

Bell, Horace. **On the Old West Coast.** 1930

Biberman, Herbert. **Salt of the Earth.** 1965

Casteñeda, Carlos E., trans. **The Mexican Side of the Texas Revolution (1836).** 1928

Casteñeda, Carlos E. **Our Catholic Heritage in Texas, 1519-1936.** Seven volumes. 1936-1958

Colton, Walter. **Three Years in California.** 1850

Cooke, Philip St. George. **The Conquest of New Mexico and California.** 1878

Cue Canovas, Agustin. **Los Estados Unidos Y El Mexico Olvidado.** 1970

Curtin, L. S. M. **Healing Herbs of the Upper Rio Grande.** 1947

Fergusson, Harvey. **The Blood of the Conquerors.** 1921

Fernandez, Jose. **Cuarenta Años de Legislador:** Biografia del Senador Casimiro Barela. 1911

Francis, Jessie Davies. **An Economic and Social History of Mexican California** (1822-1846). Volume I: Chiefly Economic. Two vols. in one. 1976

Getty, Harry T. **Interethnic Relationships in the Community of Tucson.** 1976

Guzman, Ralph C. **The Political Socialization of the Mexican American People.** 1976

Harding, George L. **Don Agustin V. Zamorano.** 1934

Hayes, Benjamin. **Pioneer Notes from the Diaries of Judge Benjamin Hayes, 1849-1875.** 1929

Herrick, Robert. **Waste.** 1924

Jamieson, Stuart. **Labor Unionism in American Agriculture.** 1945

Landolt, Robert Garland. **The Mexican-American Workers of San Antonio, Texas.** 1976

Lane, Jr., John Hart. **Voluntary Associations Among Mexican Americans in San Antonio, Texas.** 1976

Livermore, Abiel Abbot. **The War with Mexico Reviewed.** 1850

Loyola, Mary. **The American Occupation of New Mexico, 1821-1852.** 1939

Macklin, Barbara June. **Structural Stability and Culture Change in a Mexican-American Community.** 1976

McWilliams, Carey. **Ill Fares the Land:** Migrants and Migratory Labor in the United States. 1942

Murray, Winifred. **A Socio-Cultural Study of 118 Mexican Families Living in a Low-Rent Public Housing Project in San Antonio, Texas.** 1954

Niggli, Josephina. **Mexican Folk Plays.** 1938

Parigi, Sam Frank. **A Case Study of Latin American Unionization in Austin, Texas.** 1976

Poldervaart, Arie W. **Black-Robed Justice.** 1948

Rayburn, John C. and Virginia Kemp Rayburn, eds. **Century of Conflict, 1821-1913.** Incidents in the Lives of William Neale and William A. Neale, Early Settlers in South Texas. 1966

Read, Benjamin. **Illustrated History of New Mexico.** 1912

Rodriguez, Jr., Eugene. **Henry B. Gonzalez.** 1976

Sanchez, Nellie Van de Grift. **Spanish and Indian Place Names of California.** 1930

Sanchez, Nellie Van de Grift. **Spanish Arcadia.** 1929

Shulman, Irving. **The Square Trap.** 1953

Tireman, L. S. **Teaching Spanish-Speaking Children.** 1948

Tireman, L. S. and Mary Watson. **A Community School in a Spanish-Speaking Village.** 1948

Twitchell, Ralph Emerson. **The History of the Military Occupation of the Territory of New Mexico.** 1909

Twitchell, Ralph Emerson. **The Spanish Archives of New Mexico.** Two vols. 1914

U. S. House of Representatives. **California and New Mexico:** Message from the President of the United States, January 21, 1850. 1850

Valdes y Tapia, Daniel. **Hispanos and American Politics.** 1976

West, Stanley A. **The Mexican Aztec Society.** 1976

Woods, Frances Jerome. **Mexican Ethnic Leadership in San Antonio, Texas.** 1949